ROBERT E. LEE

COMMANDERS IN FOCUS

ROBERT E. LEE

PHILIP KATCHER

BRASSEY'S

General Robert E. Lee, C.S.A.,
1865. (Mathew Brady Collection)

First published in 2004 by Brassey's

An imprint of Chrysalis Books Group

Brassey's
The Chrysalis Building, Bramley Road,
London W10 6SP

Distributed in North America by
Casemate Publishing, 2114 Darby Road,
Havertown, PA 19083, USA

Philip Katcher has asserted his moral right
to be identified as the author of this work.

British Library Cataloguing in Publication Data
A catalogue record for this book is available
from the British Library

Library of Congress Cataloging in Publication Data
available

ISBN 1 85753 377 1

Photograph acknowledgements as caption credits;
other illustrations via PageantPix.

Edited and designed by DAG Publications Ltd
Designed by David Gibbons
Edited by Michael Boxall
Cartography and layout by Anthony A. Evans

Printed in Singapore.

CONTENTS

INTRODUCTION

Robert E. Lee commanded a single army in a local war and, in the end, he lost. This would seem to put him on a par with such other 19th-century generals as Mexico's Santa Anna de López, Russia's Prince Alexander Sergeievich Menshikov, Austria's General Gyulai, Denmark's Lieutenant-General C. J. de Mesa, and France's General Elie F. Forey. Their names don't ring many bells today, but the name of Robert E. Lee still resonates. His face has adorned the postage stamps of the nation he fought against. His grave is a shrine in the centre of the college he headed after his surrender at Appomattox. His character has been favourably depicted in several motion pictures. People to this day buy expensive prints and other souvenirs that feature him.

Lee came to fame naturally. His father had been a distinguished general during the War of American Independence, leading a group known as 'Lee's Light Horse' in the southern theatre of that war. In later years he had financial problems and suffered ill health after a brawl. He was absent from home for some time, so Lee grew up largely under the influence of his mother, and, while still a youth, the family had to quit their distinguished home for more modest housing in Alexandria, Virginia.

None the less, Lee was bound for a military career; his brother Sydney Smith chose the navy. Distinguished in his studies at the U.S. Military Academy in West Point and then the Mexican–American War, where he caught the eye of the Army's General-in-Chief, Winfield Scott, Lee had an outstanding career up to the outbreak of the Civil War and the secession of his native state of Virginia from the Union. His abilities had caught the eye of Jefferson Davis, a politician and former U.S. Army officer, when he was named Secretary of War. When Davis formed a new 2nd Cavalry Regiment he staffed it largely with Southern officers whom he had noted, and Lee was nominated lieutenant colonel of the regiment. Having been a staff officer in the Corps of Engineers until now, it was quite a jump to be given a higher rank in the cavalry, and when the Civil War broke out he was being considered for high U.S. Army command. But in the interests of his home state, he forsook his career, and the constitution he had long ago sworn to defend, although he seems to have experienced some conflict in making this decision, for practical reasons if for nothing else; he was by no means certain that the South would prevail against the overwhelming numerical and economic strength of the United States.

In 1861, when the Federal government, headed by President Abraham Lincoln, called upon the states to provide volunteers to suppress the rebellion of some Southern states, Virginia's government refused to supply its quota. Instead delegates to a state convention voted to take the state out of the Union and join with fellow Southern states in a new Confederate States of America. Lee was offered command of the state forces of Virginia, while his brother joined Virginia's new navy as its leader. Although Lee had yet to resign his U.S. Army commission, he accepted a position as major general in command of Virginia's forces. When Virginia joined the new Confederacy, Richmond, its capital city and a major industrial area in an otherwise agrarian region, was chosen as the site of its new national capital. Virginia's forces were absorbed into those of the Confederate States, and Lee was placed on the list of the five individuals from the pre-war U.S. Army who were named brigadier generals in the Regular Army of the Confederacy.

The new country's Regular Army was small; both sides would fight the war with largely state-organised units made up originally of volunteers and later by a mix of volunteers and conscripts. On the Confederate side, in the war in northern Virginia in which Lee fought, there was essentially no Regular Confederate Army presence. Lee would have to deal with volunteers after a lifetime of dealing with regular officers and enlisted men. Moreover, consistently the forces under his command were smaller than those of the enemy who could draw on a much larger population base. The fact that most of the battles Lee fought were between forces roughly equal in terms of fighting men available on each side is due more to U.S. Army high command ineptitude than the Confederacy's inability to recruit, train, and equip armies equal in size to those of the United States.

Lee's home in Arlington, Stratford. It was quickly captured by Federal forces, seen in this photograph, and used as a graveyard for their dead. It is now the site of Arlington National Cemetery.

The Confederacy lacked the industrial and agricultural base to provide its volunteers with the weapons, uniforms, and food it needed. Confederate troops relied on imported *matériel*, uniforms and cloth, and even food brought into Southern ports. At the outset the small U.S. Navy was unable to blockade these ports completely, but as it enlarged, supplies flowing into the South dwindled. While planters replaced their cotton crops with corn, wheat, and the like, a handful of Southern entrepreneurs opened factories to produce weapons, accoutrements and uniforms for Southern soldiers, but their output would never come close to that of the Northern manufacturers and farmers.

Lee had one advantage: The armies of the Confederacy were fighting a defensive war. The South had to be marched over, the flag of the United States placed above state and local capitals throughout the South in order for the North to prevail. Moreover, Lee's men were fighting in their own backyards for their own homes, while the Northern troops had to march south to conquer alien territory, their sole motivation being the retention of a democratic government, which was a fairly abstract notion. This advantage was somewhat offset by the fact that the Confederate government decided on a policy of defending every inch of its territory, even land that was not yet threatened. This meant that large pockets of Southern troops spent most of the war garrisoning cities and areas that were not attacked until the end, which reduced the number of men available for service in armies such as Lee's that were actually doing most of the marching and fighting.

Lee seems to have been a man born out of his time: the last 18th-century man fighting a 19th-century war against a 20th-century leader, U. S. Grant. Although he had been educated at the expense of the United States and spent long years in the service of that country, when it came time to take sides, he went with romantic thought and decided to serve his local government rather than the national one.

EARLY CAREER

Robert Edward Lee was born to a distinguished family on 19 January 1807. His father was the famous War of American Independence cavalry commander 'Light Horse Harry' Lee; his mother, Ann Carter Lee, was from the distinguished Carter family of Virginia. He was born in Stratford, a manor house, but would not live there long. His father, after the war, plunged into schemes to get rich through real estate purchases on the frontier and, in fact, was not present when his son Robert was born. In 1809 his father was arrested for debt and was thereafter in jail for a year. The family moved to Alexandria, a town on the northern Virginia border across the Potomac River from the new national capital of Washington, D.C.

Lee's father had been against waging the War of 1812 and befriended a newspaper editor in Georgetown who agreed with his stance. When a mob came to destroy this editor's press, old soldier Light Horse joined the fight, only to receive a terrible beating. Although he survived, he was an invalid until he died six years later. At the time, 25 March 1818, he was on a ship bound from Savannah, Georgia, back to Virginia, and his body was put ashore on Dungeness, Cumberland Island, Georgia, where he was buried. It would take a year for the family to learn of his fate.

Despite his father's disgrace, Lee came to believe that he was of the upper class, related to a much earlier upper-class Lee family in England, knowing that his great-great-grandfather, Richard Lee, had owned some 16,000 acres of land in Virginia at his death in 1663–64. Indeed, by 1659 the Lees of Virginia had taken for their own the arms of a branch of the Lees of Shropshire, England. As a result, Lee fancied himself a descendant of English nobility, cavaliers, something that inspired him with a constant sense of *noblesse oblige*.

Young Robert entered a free school, the Alexandria Academy, where he studied for three years until graduating. The family tradition of military service beckoned. His elder brother Sidney Smith was already in the U.S. Navy, so Robert was destined for the Army. On 7 February 1824 family counsellor, William H. Fitzhugh wrote to the Secretary of War asking that Lee be appointed to the U.S. Military Academy in West Point, New York. 'An intimate acquaintance, & a constant intercourse with him, almost from his infancy, authorise me to speak in the most unqualified terms of his amiable disposition, & his correct and gentlemanly habits,' Fitzhugh wrote. 'He is disposed to devote himself to the profession of arms.'

To prepare himself for the course of study at the Academy, which was designed to produce trained engineers to build the new republic, Lee entered a local school to brush up on higher mathematics. His professor there noted: 'He was a most exemplary pupil in every respect. He was never behind time in his studies; never failed in a single recitation; was perfectly observant of the rules and regulations of the institution; was gentlemanly, unobtrusive, and respectful in all his deportment to his teacher and his fellow-students. His speciality was *finishing up*. He imparted a finish and neatness, as he proceeded, to everything he undertook.'

Lee was appointed a cadet at the Academy on 17 March 1825. There he was plunged into an academic programme that centred on mathematics and French, the former for engineering and the latter to be able to read the advanced texts in use. During his first year this was all that was taught, the mathematics including algebra, geometry, and trigonometry. In the second year he received training in drawing and analytical and descriptive geometry. The third year schedule included physics (natural and experimental philosophy), chemistry, and topographical drawing. The final year's subjects included engineering, rhetoric, an introduction to the moral and political sciences, and, finally, the 'science of war'. This latter course especially stressed the strategy and tactics of the world's most recent great period of fighting, the Napoleonic Wars. Many of the lessons were drawn from a French text, *The Art of War*, by a Napoleonic officer, Baron Antoine Henri de Jomini.

Jomini's book divided war into five aspects: strategy, grand tactics, logistics, engineering and tactics, while also noting the importance of diplomacy in relation to war. He then analysed strategic problems in different theatres and on different types of terrain, tactics of attack and defence, of surprise and turning manoeuvres, and special operations, and reconnaissance, and the deployment of military forces. Examples were drawn from Napoleonic battles fought by large masses of men, in close formations, fighting with short-range, smoothbore flintlock muskets. This book, however, would form the basis for Lee's understanding of military strategy and tactics.

The cadets also received four hours' drill a day and, for third and fourth classmen, dancing lessons to polish their social graces, many of them having come from a frontier background.

While Lee was a cadet the Academy came under fire from politicians, especially Andrew Jackson, a president of the people's class, from a western state, who came into office in 1828. Jackson disapproved of the strict military discipline of the Academy, whose superintendent, Sylvanus Thayer, had cadets dismissed for infractions such as being caught drinking. This was a problem; on 4 July of the year Lee entered the academy, during the annual celebration of American independence, cadets staged a drunken and near riotous exhibition. Thayer immediately ruled that no more alcohol would be served to cadets on the post for any reason. Instead many cadets sneaked off the post to a nearby tavern, the well-known Benny Havens, from time to time, facing demerits if caught. Any cadet who received more than 200 demerits in an academic year would be automatically dismissed.

Lee, however, managed to stay above these infractions of discipline, including the notorious 'Egg-Nog Riot' of Christmas Eve, 1826, which involved a number of fellow cadets of Southern birth. Indeed, Lee set a record by graduating second in the Class of 1829 without a single demerit on his sheet. His was such a calm, obedient demeanour that fellow cadets nicknamed him 'The Marble Man' or the 'Marble Model'. Highest academic standing in the class was achieved by Cadet Charles Mason from New York, who resigned from the U.S. Army in 1831 to take up the profession of law, eventually becoming the president of several railroads, and would not see any Civil War service. Lee's academic work was so outstanding that he was named an acting assistant professor of mathematics at the Academy while in his final year.

Lee had entered a distinguished company at the Academy. Joseph Eggleston Johnston, who would become one of the Confederacy's leading generals, was a cadet in the same class. Jefferson Davis, who would become the Confederacy's president, was a year ahead of him. Leonidas Polk, who resigned from the Army shortly after graduating to become an Episcopal priest, only to join the Confederate Army as a lieutenant general in the western theatre, was two years ahead of him. Albert Sidney Johnston, whom Davis felt to be the Confederacy's best general, was in the senior class when Lee entered the Academy. William Nelson Pendleton, who would later serve as Lee's chief of artillery and rector of his church after the war, entered the Academy a year after Lee. John Bankhead Magruder, a divisional commander during Lee's attack in the Seven Days battles, was in Pendleton's class. Several important U.S. Army leaders during the Civil War were also in the Academy during Lee's stay there.

While Lee usually portrayed a calm, almost forbidding appearance to many who knew him only slightly, with his friends as early as at the Academy Lee proved that he had a humorous side as well. For example he wrote to a friend, whom he called 'Sir Richard', during this time, giving him instructions on his behaviour: '... 1. Not to go mad from Joy or Drink ... 2. to eschew all types of communication ... 6. get Miss Hollie, or Virginia Mason to ride out to Arlington with him. When he arrives in the district, or any other pretty girl will do as well ... 7. Sometimes think of R. E. Lee.'

Upon graduation, given his high standing in the class, Lee was given his choice of the branch of service in which he would serve. As usual when given such a choice, he picked the Corps of Engineers, but at this time there were no enlisted engineers in the army, so his would always be a staff position rather than in command of troops in the field. All was not joyous for him, because his mother died in the summer after his graduation.

While putting affairs in order at home, he received his first assignment, to Cockspur Island, in the Savannah River, Georgia, to work on a heavy fort planned to be built there. His next assignment was to Old Port, Virginia, to complete work on Fort Monroe. While there he married a distant kinswoman, Mary Custis, on 30 June 1831. The couple would have seven children over the course of fourteen years, although she rarely left Virginia to accompany him to distant posts.

Just after her wedding she became ill, remaining in poor health through that summer, and indeed was an invalid for much of the rest of her life. On 22 February 1832 she noted in her diary, 'How sad & depressed with bodily indisposition on which my mind continually dwells.' Lee displayed his concern but resignation to the will of his God when he wrote to her from Savannah on 8 February 1862, 'Take good care of yourself & be resigned to what God ordains for us.'

Despite her indispositions and a marriage that does not appear to have been a very happy one, she was a constant source of support and help throughout his life. During the Civil War she spent much of her time knitting garments for the soldiers; this was in Richmond, the family home in Alexandria having been occupied by U.S. troops early on. On 2 May 1864, Lee wrote, 'Your note of Saturday dear Mary with the bag of socks arrived yesterday, I distributed the socks to the Stonewall Brigade which makes 392 sent to those troops. I am much obliged to you for the shirt & collars. They look very nice.'

While Lee was at Fort Monroe there was a slave uprising in nearby Southampton. Although he did not participate in putting down the insurrection, in which some 60 whites were killed, the post was placed on alert, African-Americans were forbidden to enter, and the garrison was reinforced by artillery and infantry. But promotions in the peacetime army were few and Lee's career seemed to stall. In February 1837 Lee wrote a friend, 'You ask what are my prospects in the Corps? Bad enough – unless it is increased and something done for us, and then perhaps they will be better. As to what I intend doing, it is rather hard to answer. There is one thing certain, I must get away from here, nor can I consent to stay any longer than the rising of Cong[ress]. I should have made a desperate effort last spring, but Mary's health was so bad I could not have left her, and she could not have gone with me. I am waiting, looking and hoping for some good opportunity to bid an affectionate farewell to my Uncle Sam …'

Lee's opportunity to get away from Fort Monroe and the work he'd been doing in the engineer office at Washington, D.C., finally came when he volunteered for a job that had just opened on the Mississippi River in St. Louis, Missouri, in 1837. Mary did not accompany him, and he wrote home, 'Oh, what pleasure I lose in being separated from my children. Nothing can compensate me for that, still I must remain here, ready to perform what little service I can, and hope for the best.' He came home in late 1837, partly on leave and partly to get engineering supplies from Washington, and in March 1838 when he returned to St. Louis his family came with him. That summer he was promoted to captain of engineers.

In December 1838 Lee learned that one of his mentors, General Charles Gratiot, the army's chief engineer, had been dismissed from the service under a cloud, having taken treasury money he claimed was due to him as commissions and allowances. Lee was shocked, writing, 'I believe the news of his death would have been less painful to me.' Lee gathered material in his office and went to Washington to come to Gratiot's aid, but to no avail. Joseph G. Totten, a colonel of engineers with whom Lee had had no working relationship, became the army's new chief engineer.

In 1839 the family returned to Virginia, where Mary gave birth, after which Lee went back to St. Louis alone. In 1840 he returned to duty in Washington, from where he was sent to inspect three forts on the North Carolina coastline. In 1841 he was reassigned to engineer work on forts in New York Harbour, where he settled his family for the time being.

In 1844 he was sent to attend the final examinations of cadets at West Point, and became more closely acquainted with Major General Winfield Scott, a hero of the War of 1812 and now general-in-chief of the U.S. Army. This was to have a most important influence on his career. Lee also had time to serve as a vestry-man in the Episcopal Church at Fort Hamilton, New York, where he was based this time. Throughout his life the teachings of the Episcopal Church played a large role in his life style, thought, and behaviour. While insistent on all the trap-pings of the military life, he declined to take part in the controversy that plagued the Church, starting when the Anglo-Catholic Oxford Movement began to push for a return to earlier rituals and beliefs. He remained a 'low church' or evangel-ical Episcopalian all his life, and one who bent over backwards to avoid becom-ing involved in personal conflicts.

In 1844 Lee returned to duty in Washington to serve as assistant to the chief engineer. There he learned how much he disliked all the paperwork involved, writing to a friend on 18 March 1845, 'Could you see my list of correspondents among whigs, democrats, congressmen and officers, you would [not] wonder at my horror at the sight of pen, ink and paper, and with what perfect disgust I pick up my hat between 4 and 5 P.M. with the firm determination of doing nothing until the next morning, except to go home, eat my dinner, play with the little Lees and rest. At 8 next morning I am again in the saddle to go through the same routine.' This dislike of paperwork would follow him into army command.

Lee's days in an office were numbered, however. During the evening of 9 May 1846, President James K. Polk received a dispatch 'from General Taylor by the Southern mail which had just arrived, giving information that a part of the Mexican army had crossed the Del Norte and attacked and killed and captured two companies of dragoons of General Taylor's army consisting of 63 officers and men … I immediately summoned the Cabinet to meet at half-past seven o'clock this evening … The Cabinet were unanimously of opinion, and it was so agreed, that a message should be sent to Congress on Monday laying all the information in my possession before them and recommending vigorous and prompt measures to enable the executive to prosecute the war.'

The United States was at war, and wars made careers. Captain Lee wanted to get out of the office and into the field. On 19 August 1846, Lee received orders to report to Brigadier General John E. Wool, then in San Antonio de Bexar, Texas, at the front. He quickly closed his accounts, made his will, and boarded a ship for the south. He reached San Antonio on 21 September. Wool had been ordered there in July to prepare an expedition against Chihauhua, Mexico, made up of two companies of the 6th U.S. Infantry, two companies of the 11th U.S. Dragoons, a battery from the 4th U.S. Artillery, a squadron of dragoons, a regiment of volunteer cavalry from Arkansas, and the 1st and 2nd Illinois Volunteer Infantry Regiments. The engineer officer already on his staff was Captain William D. Fraser, who had graduated first in his U.S. Military Academy Class of 1834.

Lee arrived just in time for action, the column heading off at the end of September. They reached the Rio Grande, the river separating Mexico and Texas, on 8 October, one eye-witness noting, 'it being accomplished in this time by the aid of the indefatigable exertions of those distinguished officers Captains Lee and Frazier, [sic] of the corps of engineers, they having prepared the way with a pioneer company, by levelling hills, filling ravines, making bridges, &c.'

This pioneer company, Lee's first actual field command after many years of Army service, was made up of volunteers taken from different infantry units rather than trained engineer troops. Seeing how well this company worked under the direction of professional engineers would cause Lee in later years to fail to see the need of trained enlisted engineer units. His opponent in the Civil War, the Army of the Potomac, used both Regular Army companies of enlisted engineer troops and specially recruited specialist volunteer engineer regiments. However, his own Army of Northern Virginia would use pioneer companies very much like the one he directed in Wool's force under supervision of officer members of the Corps of Engineers. It was not until late in the war that he was forced by the Secretary of War to accept the use of regular, trained engineer companies.

Lee and Fraser supervised the building of a pontoon bridge across the river, and on 12 October, the bridge completed, Wool's column crossed into Mexico. After an uneventful march, they reached Monclova, a town of some 8,000 inhabitants, on the 30th. There they would remain for almost three weeks while awaiting an armistice earlier arranged between U.S. Major General Zachary Taylor and his Mexican opponents. On 24 November Wool, who had been ordered to move towards Taylor, leaving five companies of Illinois volunteers to garrison Monclova, headed south again. They soon reached Parras, some 365 miles south of the border. Again they met no opposition on the way.

The force halted there until, on 17 December, Wool was ordered to reinforce the garrison at Saltillo, threatened by attack. Wool moved out quickly and covered a hundred miles in four days, reaching the U.S. camp near Agua Neuva, a little south of Saltillo. As it turned out, no attack was made on the American position, and the troops settled down. Fraser was recalled, leaving Lee as Wool's senior staff engineer. Wool also named him assistant inspector-general on Wool's staff.

Continued rumours of forthcoming Mexican attacks caused Wool's force to be sent first to Encantada and then to Buena Vista. At camp there Lee was in Taylor's headquarters when a young officer rode up saying that he had seen 20,000 troops with 250 cannon moving on the camp. Taylor asked if the officer had seen this with his own eyes, to which the officer replied that he had.

'Captain,' the ever-calm Taylor replied, 'if you say you saw it, of course I must believe you; but I would not have believed it if I had seen it myself.'

This calm response to excited reports of enemy numbers and movements made a deep impression on Lee. Years later when he was in command of the Army of Northern Virginia at Chancellorsville, he replied to those bearing him news of huge advancing Union forces with Taylor's words.

Another incident here further impressed the value of remaining calm in the face of rumoured enemy attacks. On Christmas morning dust from an American patrol caused alarms to be raised in camp, while men at the front reported a row of white objects in the distance that were, they said, tents of the Mexican Army. Lee rode out to discover that the objects were a flock of sheep bedded down in the moonlit night.

On 16 January 1847, Lee received orders to leave Wool's staff and join that of the new main American army, under General-in-Chief Winfield Scott, which was bound for Vera Cruz, there to march up the National Road and take Mexico City itself. Lee left the next morning and rode to Brazos where Scott's army was preparing for the expedition. There he was reunited with his old classmate Joseph Johnston, Corps of Topographical Engineers, with whom he would share a cabin on the trip south. Pierre G. T. Beauregard was another engineer officer on Scott's staff, all under direct supervision of the army's chief engineer, Joseph Totten. On 15 February, Scott and his staff left Brazos for Tampico where his troops were waiting to board ships for the voyage to Vera Cruz. They left Tampico on the 20th, Scott and his staff on the *Massachusetts*. After a short stay on Lobos Island, they arrived off Vera Cruz on 5 March.

On the 9th Scott's army poured into boats and landed, unopposed, on Mexican soil, not far from the fortified city of Vera Cruz. While the troops were landing, the infantry were deployed for defence and cannon and supplies came ashore. Scott held a meeting with what he called his 'little cabinet', made up of Totten, Lee, his acting inspector-general and his acting adjutant-general to discuss, he later wrote, 'storming parties and regular siege approaches'. The staff actually landed next day and examined the Mexican position. Fearing high cost of human life if the city were directly attacked, Scott determined to set up a formal siege and Lee and other engineers went to work laying out and super- vising the digging of trenches.

One evening Lee and Beauregard were making their way back to the main lines from an advanced working-party when a nervous sentry fired on them before receiving a reply to his call of, 'Who goes there?' The ball passed between Lee's left arm and body, singeing his uniform. Although Lee later pleaded for leniency, Scott insisted that the sentry be punished.

Lee laid out a battery of naval cannon, which was ready for action on 24 March. That evening the battery opened fire, the first time Lee had ever directed fire on an enemy. He later wrote home that the fire 'was terrific, and the shells thrown from our battery were constant and regular discharges, so beautiful in their flight and so destructive in their fall. It was awful! My heart bled for the inhabitants. The soldiers I did not care so much for, but it was terrible to think of the women and children.'

The battery continued to fire until the 26th when a Mexican flag of truce was sent out from the city asking for terms of surrender. The Mexicans rejected the terms Scott first proposed, but a second version was favourably received. It called for the Mexicans to march out of the city with the honours of war, to surrender their arms, and then accept parole not to fight again against U.S. forces until properly exchanged. Lee and Johnston were sent into Vera Cruz, the first Americans to enter the city, to settle the final terms of surrender. An eye-witness noted, 'They were then distinguished young officers, intimate friends to each other, and their martial appearance as they rode, superbly mounted, to meet the Mexican officers, gave a general feeling of satisfaction to our army, that such representatives of the "North Americas" had been chosen for such an occasion.'

On 29 March the Mexican troops left the city and the Americans went in. They were not to stay there long, however, because the yellow fever season was at hand, and Scott wanted to get his troops out of the region. So he began sending out units up the National Road towards Mexico City, leaving the city himself with his staff on 12 April. On the 14th they reached an enemy defensive position drawn up in a mountain pass on the Plan del Rio. Cannon frowned down on the Americans from every high point. Scott sent Lee to reconnoitre the enemy position. On the 15th Lee examined the positions, especially around a conical hill called Cerro Gordo, and found them to be well laid out indeed and defended by considerably more troops than Scott had on hand. On the Mexican left flank, however, he found a way around the line, himself being almost captured as he appeared in the enemy rear and had to hide behind a log as Mexican soldiers passed by.

When Lee returned, Scott ordered him to take a working-party and cut a trail large enough for the entire army to use. By the end of the 16th the job was done. The last troops in Scott's army finally reached the field on the 18th, and Scott then had most of them demonstrate against the Mexican front while Lee led a division around his new trail and against Cerro Gordo. On 19 April Scott was able to report: 'The plan of attack … was finely executed by this gallant army before two o'clock P.M., yesterday. We are quite embarrassed with the results of victory – prisoners of war, heavy ordnance, field batteries, small arms, and accoutrements. About 3,000 men laid down their arms, with the usual proportion of field and company officers, besides five generals, several of them of great distinction – Pinson, Jarreo, La Vega, Noriega, and Obando. A sixth general, Vasquez, was killed in defending the battery (tower) in the rear of the line of defence, the capture of which gave us those glorious results.' On 23 April, Scott added: 'I am compelled to make special mention of the services of Captain R. E. Lee, Engineer. This officer, greatly distinguished at the siege of Vera Cruz, was again indefatigable, during these operations, in reconnaissances as daring as laborious, and of the utmost value. Nor was he less conspicuous [sic] in planting batteries, and in conducting columns to their stations under the heavy fire of the enemy.' Lee's important participation in the battle would bring him the brevet rank of major on 24 August.

The decision to split an army smaller than that of the enemy, and send a part of it around an enemy flank would be one Lee, who saw how well it worked at Cerro Gordo, would make for himself at Chancellorsville in future years.

Scott wasted no time after the battle, pressing on to get out of the area affected by yellow fever, of which the cause was unknown at the time. Jalapa, a city of some 5,000 inhabitants, fell on the 19th and Perote quickly thereafter. Scott pushed a division forward to Puebla, which fell on 15 May, after a mere skirmish with defending Mexican cavalry. The army was now only 93 miles from Mexico City. Scott set up his headquarters at Puebla on the 28th.

Here he had to wait as volunteers who had enlisted for only a year's service were sent home and reinforcements, who had to be drilled after their arrival,

Major General Winfield Scott at Vera Cruz, 25 March 1847. Copy of lithograph by Nathaniel Currier, 1847.

arrived to take their place. Lee spent this time with Major William Turnbull, Scott's chief topographical engineer, making a map of possible approaches to Mexico City. When all the reinforcements had arrived, Scott decided virtually to abandon his line of communications and supplies between the army and Vera Cruz, rather than waste his strength by garrisoning every post between the two, and boldly cut loose for Mexico City. Lee would make a similar move in his 1863 raid into Pennsylvania, although his lines of communication south were never fully severed any more than Scott's were to the sea.

On 10 August Scott's army set off, moving by divisions, no division ever being more than eight miles or a five-hour march from another, if needed for support in case of a Mexican attack. On the 11th Scott stopped at Ayotla, the last town between Vera Cruz and Mexico City. Between his army and its goal lay marshy territory across which a causeway between Lake Texcoco and Lakes Xichimilco and Chalco was the only viable route to the city. This, intelligence revealed, was strongly held by Mexican forces. Again Lee was sent to reconnoitre. He reported that the main Mexican works were based on a hill commanding the area called El Penon. Before one reached that point, however, a road branched off to the left crossing through a village known as Mexicalcingo, also fortified with enemy artillery.

Scott wanted to avoid a bloody battle, so as to conserve his army's strength for what he reckoned would be a costly fight later for Mexico City itself. While he was considering his choices, word arrived from one of his divisional commanders that his staff officers had found a way around the lower end of Lake Chalco that would allow the army to move on the city from the south and avoid all the defensive works to his front. Scott ordered the army to take this route, sending Lee ahead to reconnoitre the roads. At the same time he realised that such a march would not be a secret for long, and that the Mexicans would probably move to block the Americans at San Augustin. The land there was ideal for defence, with ground too soft for wheeled vehicles to its east and hardened slabs of lava to the west, also impassable for wheeled vehicles. The only glimmer of hope came from a road that led to Churubusco, around San Augustin, and back to the Acapulco–Mexico City highway.

Lee, given command of the 11th Infantry and two dragoon companies, was sent to check out this road, while another engineer was sent to examine the road directly to San Augustin. Lee reached the top of Zacatepec and saw that the Mexicans were well prepared for battle on the San Angel road, and were fortifying a hill near the village of Padierna. A skirmish with Mexican troops there convinced him that if the Mexicans were able to use the road he had reconnoitred, so too could the U.S. Army after some work on it was put in hand. He argued for this approach that night at a council of war Scott held, while the

SCOTT'S MEXICAN CAMPAIGN, MARCH TO SEPTEMBER 1847

engineer who had studied the main road argued for an attack directly on San Antonio, using a flank movement only a short distance into the lava beds on the west. U.S. Navy Lieutenant Raphael Semmes, present at the conference, later noted: 'The services of Captain Lee were invaluable to his chief. Endowed with a mind which has no superior in his corps, and possessing great energy of character, he examined, counselled, and advised with a judgement, tact, and discretion worthy of all praise. His talent for topography was peculiar, and he seemed to receive impressions intuitively, which it cost other men much labour to acquire.'

After the meeting broke up, Scott directed Lee to take a company of engineers up the San Angel road at the head of a division for protection and prepare it for use by the main attack force. By early afternoon on 19 August, the road builders had progressed to a point where Mexican fortifications, complete with 22 cannon, blocked their way. American artillery was brought up and sited under Lee and a couple of other staff engineers. In the exchange of artillery fire that followed Lee was standing next to Preston Johnston, nephew of his friend Joseph Johnston, when the young man was fatally wounded, a shell having taken off one of his legs.

A stream flowing through a deep ravine separated the two sides. Mexican artillery took its toll as the Americans brought up their infantry. The Americans had to react quickly, and they decided to pass west, through the pedregal, the local name for lava beds, and turn the Mexican left flank. Several brigades, some 3,300 strong, made this trip and reached the village of San Geronimo a mile north of the Mexican position. On the other side they could see another group of Mexican troops which they estimated at some 12,000. Luckily for the Americans darkness set in before this force could attack the American brigades now cut off from Scott's headquarters. A heavy, cold rain fell on the miserable troops, who had no shelter and little firewood.

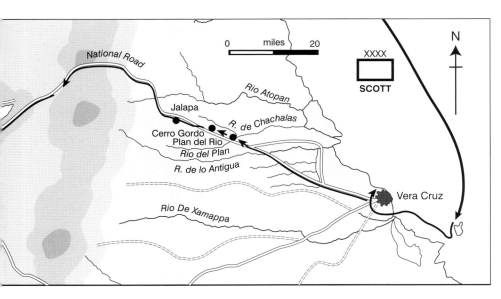

As the troops huddled and tried to keep warm and dry, the commander of the isolated brigades determined to attack the next morning and told Lee to so inform Scott. Lee started off at about 8 p.m., making his way cautiously through unknown territory where stray Mexican units possibly lurked, and reached Scott's headquarters at about 11 p.m. He then guided one of Scott's divisional commanders back to the American lines on the pedregal, where he passed on Scott's orders calling for a demonstration to help the attacking force the next morning. Although it was now 1 a.m., Lee pressed on to another brigade head-quarters to guide those troops to the advanced American battery position. As they reached their position, the American attack struck and completely routed the Mexicans.

Lee went out to the newly captured position, where he met Joseph Johnston, who was mourning his nephew's death. He then returned to Scott's headquarters, where he met the general who was on his way to the battlefield. Scott hurried his men on, having found that their advance had been so sudden and so over-whelming that the Mexicans had abandoned San Antonio and were retreating towards their next line of defence at Churubusco where the bridge and the convent of San Mateo formed their strongpoints there.

Scott's forces struck this position, one brigade enveloping the convent on the right. Lee positioned a howitzer battery to smash the head of the Mexican column. The Mexican right was on boggy ground that could not be crossed easily, so a frontal assault, combined with the success on their left was the only option left, and in heavy fighting the Americans carried the position. Hotly pursued, the Mexican troops fled to the gates of Mexico City.

In their reports, the U.S. commanders heaped great praise on Lee, who had been active for 36 hours non-stop. One of them noted: 'His reconnaissances, though pushed far beyond the bounds of prudence, were conduced with so much skill, that their fruits were of utmost value – the soundness of his judge-ment and personal daring being equally conspicuous.' Scott himself said that Lee's two trips in the darkness over the pedregal on 16–17 August made up 'the greatest feat of physical and moral courage performed by any individual, in my knowledge, throughout the campaign.'

What Lee must have learned from this campaign was that audacity, actively pressed, even against large odds, would bring success.

Scott's army now rested at the very walls of Mexico's capital city. The Mexicans requested a truce in order to discuss peace terms. A civilian commissioner autho-rised to draw up a peace treaty was at Scott's headquarters. On 24 August 1847, a truce was agreed and Lee took advantage of this time to rest in the resort town of Tacubaya. The truce was to end on 7 September, and in the evening of the 6th, no real progress having been made, Scott called his staff to discuss attacking the city. Lee, now chief engineer in the absence of Major Scott who was ill, was given the job of reconnoitring the approaches to the city. His observations of active defensive preparations prompted Scott to make his own reconnaissance on the 9th.

Scott held a council of war on 10 September and two plans were discussed. Lee's favoured an attack by way of the southern gates. Others, notably fellow engineer Beauregard, spoke in favour of attacking Chapultepec and the city's western gates. The idea being that its capture would be easy after a day's bombardment. Scott came down on the side of the Chapultepec attack.

Lee and his fellow engineers, notably Lieutenant George B. McClellan, began siting batteries to cover the attack. Once the bombardment had begun Scott ordered Lee to lead one division in the assault on the 13th. At that point, Lee would have been sleepless for 48 hours.

Soon after Lee started off with the attacking force from Molino del Rey, the divisional commander was wounded and sent to the rear. The division, now reinforced, pressed on to capture Chapultepec. The exhausted Lee was slightly wounded in the advance, but did not bother to get medical attention before returning to Scott with his progress report. There, Scott later reported, 'he fainted from a wound and the loss of two nights' sleep at the batteries'.

After a sound night's sleep, Lee was his old self next morning. He was then sent to accompany troops to the centre of Mexico City where he watched the U.S. flag raised. Scott and his staff, resplendent in full dress uniforms, soon arrived on the scene. Although there were minor skirmishes with irregulars thereafter, the fighting was essentially over. Civilians now negotiated a peace treaty as the army took up garrison duties. Lee received the brevet of colonel for his service in the war.

After so many years' service Lee had finally fought in a war, and ended up with an enviable record. He was suddenly well known throughout the army. An artillery private stationed with his howitzer company at army headquarters in

Battle of Chapultepec, September 1847. Copy of print by J. Duthie after H. Billings.

Mexico City remembered him well, later recalling, 'Robert E. Lee, in particular, was a handsome, chivalrous cavalier, who at that time was captain and first adjutant to General Scott.' Scott was a prickly character, quick to find fault with others. He was a political opponent of his president, James K. Polk. He quarrelled with his generals, bringing charges against two of them, while one brought charges against Scott himself. In all this Lee showed another side of his character, that of peacemaker. Henry Hunt, a young artillery officer who would later command the artillery of the Army of the Potomac, wrote that Lee wanted 'to heal the differences between General Scott and some of his subordinate officers'.

Before Lee could heal these breaches, however, Scott was relieved of command. Lee wrote to his brother: 'I agree with you as to the dissensions in camp; they have clouded a bright campaign. It is a context in which neither party has anything to gain and the Army much to lose, and ought to have been avoided. The whole matter will soon be before the court, and if it be seen that there has been harshness and intemperance of language on one side, it will be evident that there had been insubordination on the other.' Lee would work hard to prevent his equally prickly Confederate generals, hugely aware of personal honour, creating the same type of problems in his own army. As it turned out, Lee was called as a witness in one of the trials that resulted, in the end, in acquittals and dropped charges.

A treaty signed, the army began to return home. Lee reached Vera Cruz on 6 June and sailed for home. He took with him a great deal of experience in commanding and fighting an army in the field, as well as seeing how strategy was determined at the army's highest level. His observations would guide him when he led his own army.

One observation was that audacity would prevail over greater numbers, although Scott's audacity achieved victories over uninspired troops whose equipment and training were inferior to Lee's eventual Union enemies. Audacity, Lee observed, was not only tactical, as fought on battlefields, but campaign-wide. Scott was extremely audacious when he cut loose from his supply lines at Vera Cruz and drove to Mexico City (no less an experienced observer than the Duke of Wellington is said to have believed that the campaign would fail). Therefore he was unconcerned about being so far from his supply points when he invaded the north in 1862 and 1863.

Lee saw how Scott would come up with an overall strategy, then leave his subordinates to follow it through, giving very little hands-on direction while battle was engaged. This worked with certain subordinates, such as T. J. Jackson, in Lee's later war, but failed him miserably in battles such as Gettysburg.

He saw too how a trained, professional staff could enable a commander to appreciate a battlefield situation without personal reconnaissance, so that detailed orders could be sent to his subordinates for specific actions. Unfortunately he failed to realise that his own staff in the Army of Northern Virginia were not the West Point-trained, experienced officers at Scott's disposal in Mexico.

Therefore he left much to a staff that was too often unable to perform the duties he expected. At the same time, his observation of infantry serving as pioneers to dig roads and entrenchments, led him to play down the need of trained professional engineer troops at a time when technology was more important than it had been in Mexico.

But he learned the importance of reconnaissance before action, and this would stand him in good stead in later battles.

He saw the success of flanking moves in battles such as Cerro Gordo and San Antonio. He would see such moves work dramatically at such battles as Chancellorsville, which makes his refusal to flank the Union army at Gettysburg on the third day, instead going for a frontal assault, difficult to understand.

Lee learned the value of fortifications by observing the well-designed Mexican works at Cerro Gordo, Padierna and Mexico City. Only the poor quality of the troops that defended these works, and their superiors' inability, enabled the Americans to overrun them. From this, too, he learned that a smaller number of soldiers with excellent morale could beat a larger number whose morale was poor.

Lee found too that politicians and the military do not mix. In his own army he would not promote politicians who had gained rank to greater rank, and, in fact, tried to keep his army free of these individuals. He vastly preferred trained professionals in the army's higher ranks, because he had seen in Mexico that these were the most trustworthy.

In Mexico he met many of the individuals who would later serve him or fight him in the Civil War. He worked most closely with George McClellan and his observations of McClellan, more accurate than McClellan's of him, enabled him for the most part to correctly anticipate his enemy's moves in 1862. He also got to know Joseph Hooker, then serving on a divisional staff, pretty well and was able to read him. Although he had met Grant, he paid him little mind and was unable to remember him later. This was unfortunate from his point of view. George Meade did not serve in the drive on Mexico City, so he was not personally knowledgeable about him either. On the Confederate side, he worked closely with P. G. T. Beauregard and, of course, his Academy roommate, Joseph Johnston.

The Mexican campaign saw little cavalry used, and he was therefore deficient in knowledge of how best to use it. Railroads, telegraphs and such technology as existed in 1861 had not been employed, and he entered the Civil War with no practical knowledge of how they would affect a campaign. The army Scott commanded was largely professional, with a scattering of volunteer troops. The men, most of whom could not find civilian employment or were on the run from the law, were recruited for a five-year enlistment and were well trained. They could be called on to do things that volunteers would have to think over first. After so many successes initially, Lee began to think his Confederates were the equal of these Mexican War regulars. Moreover, Scott's army was small, especially when compared to later Civil War armies. Grant later was amused to think: 'In view of the immense bodies of men moved on the same day over narrow roads, through dense forests and across large streams, in our late [Civil] war, it seems strange now that a body of less than three thousand men should have been broken into four columns, separated by a day's march.' Nobody learned how to manage large bodies of troops in the Mexican War.

The army returned to peacetime duties, and Lee was assigned to the board of engineers responsible for Atlantic coast defences, working out of Washington so that he was able to live at home again. In September 1848 he was ordered to nearby Baltimore, Maryland, to oversee the building of a new fort, Fort Carroll. He took his family with him, renting a house in the city for the duration of his job there. Here, in the mosquito-ridden, swampy area in which the fort was being built, he became ill with a febrile illness, probably malaria, and was forced to return to Arlington to recover. Another engineer was assigned to Fort Carroll, and in August Lee was well enough to go to Rhode Island to work on the building of new barracks and a hospital at Fort Adams. While there he was ordered to the Brooklyn Navy Yard to work on the dry-dock there, but had to request to be relieved as his malaria was still troubling him.

Finally recovered, he returned to Baltimore for the 1850–51 building season. In May 1852 he was named superintendent of the Military Academy at West Point. He arrived just as the authorities, finding new cadets often academically unready for the curriculum, changed the course of study to one lasting five years. He now found himself immersed in the thing he disliked most, long hours of administrative paperwork Again his family followed him and, as his son Custis was a cadet there, for the first time in years they were all together again.

In 1853 a new administration took office, with Franklin Pierce, who had been a general in the Mexican War and with whom Lee had close associations, becoming president. He appointed as his secretary of war, Jefferson Davis, who had been a cadet with Lee. The two were to work together well, forming the basis for the hand-in-glove team they were to become during the Civil War. While at the Academy he also met a cadet with whom he would also develop a close working relationship, J. E. B. (Jeb) Stuart. He found time from his duties to devour quite a number of books from the Academy library that would prove useful later, including works on military history, biography. law, and the science of war. During this time, too, he was confirmed into the Episcopal Church, and this was to play a large part in his life thereafter.

In 1854, following a massacre near Fort Laramie, Wyoming, Secretary Davis obtained authorisation to recruit a new regiment for frontier service, the 2nd U.S. Cavalry. One of Davis' old cadet friends, Albert Sidney Johnston, was nominated colonel in command of the regiment. Johnston had resigned from the army before the Mexican War, but during the war returned to service as the colonel of a Texas volunteer rifle regiment. He was later appointed adjutant general of Texas.

Lee was chosen as the regiment's new lieutenant colonel. He finally transferred from a staff position in the Corps of Engineers to his first line assignment, in the cavalry. He now held a field command and became accustomed to the realities of command, leading reconnaissances, and heading courts-martial that revealed to him the problems of the common soldier. In his years on the staff or at the Academy he had rarely dealt directly with common enlisted men and so this exposure would stand him in good stead in later years. Also this was a good change for him because nine officers, senior in rank or date of commission, stood between him and the army's chief engineer position so he had little chance of serious promotion. On the other hand, the army's generals and colonels were all drawing near to retirement so the line offered much better prospects. In March 1855 he made the switch.

In April he was sent to Louisville, Kentucky, to command the men of the 2nd there whose colonel was unavailable at the moment. He remained in Kentucky on court-martial duties while the regiment left for Texas, then rejoined the regiment in March 1856. He was given command of two squadrons at Camp Cooper on the Brazos River. There he met and befriended one of his new lieutenants, John Bell Hood, who would go on to serve him in the Civil War. But he found his duties there depressing without his family, writing to a friend, 'Tell Robert I cannot advise him to enter the army. It is a hard life, and he can never rise to any military eminence by serving in the army.' He did find some interest in one of Davis' experiments, using imported camels to carry men and supplies in the western deserts. He praised their 'endurance, docility, and sagacity', saying one expedition was successful because of their 'reliable services'.

In 1857 he was ordered to San Antonio to take command of the regiment in the absence of Johnston who had been recalled to Washington. There he met Major R. H. Chilton, a staff paymaster who would also serve him closely in the Civil War. That October his father-in-law died and, his wife being ill with crippling arthritis at the time, he obtained leave and returned to Arlington.

Once there he encountered new problems. His wife had become essentially an invalid, and his father-in-law's estate was in financial turmoil. He applied for two months' leave to deal with these problems, but this was insufficient and he was granted additional leave, although he was called to court-martial duty from time to time. His wife's health did not improve.

All this time the question of slavery was becoming more and more heated in the country. In October 1859 a radical abolitionist from Kansas, John Brown, led his sons and several others to Harpers Ferry, Virginia, to capture the Federal armoury there. The idea was to distribute the weapons to slaves who would rally to his side and foment a wide-spread revolt. This was something that the South feared the most. There had been several slave revolts in Virginia before and the results were terrifying to white slave owners. On 17 October 1859, when word of Brown's raid reached nearby Washington, Lee was ordered with some Marines and Lieutenant Jeb Stuart to Harpers Ferry to capture Brown and his men.

Brown's men had crossed the railway bridge from Maryland, and dashed down the hill towards the armoury, but had been forced to take cover in the fire engine house at the east of the compound, where they held a number of hostages. Lee arrived outside the town to find a Maryland militia general and four companies of Maryland militia as well as the Marines. He learned that the Virginia side was swarming with local militia and armed civilians. During the night of 17 October Lee and his men crossed the bridge and surrounded the engine house. Fearing heavy losses to the hostages if he attacked immediately, he reconnoitred and planned to attack next morning.

At seven o'clock he sent Stuart with a message calling for the surrender of those in the engine house. Stuart was told not to negotiate and if the surrender were rejected to signal Lee who would then launch an assault. The attack was to be made by Marines with fixed bayonets, without firing a shot for fear of harming the hostages.

Brown, opening the door a crack, tried to get Stuart to offer him terms that would allow himself, his men, and their hostages to go to Maryland. After some discussion, Stuart stepped aside and waved his hat to go ahead. The attack, costing several Marine casualties, lasted only three minutes before the abolitionists were taken prisoner. Four of Brown's men were killed, the thirteen hostages were hungry but unharmed.

Lee had Brown sent to Charles Town, the local county seat, under Marine guard and he and the rest of the Marines returned to Washington.

Brown's raid launched great excitement in the South. Fearing repeats of this raid, citizens began raising volunteer militia companies, getting themselves uniformed, armed, and drilled. Rumours that slave states would actually leave the Union, rather than allow abolitionists to achieve a nationwide emancipation law, spread throughout the South.

Lee's time east was coming to an end, however. On 6 February 1860, he was appointed to command the Department of Texas as a brevet colonel. On the 19th he arrived at his headquarters in San Antonio, where his duties were routine. He was now 53. His classmate Joseph Johnston was appointed the army's paymaster general with the rank of brigadier general

Photographed just before the Civil War began, Lee is seen here wearing civilian clothes. His hair turned grey and he grew a beard early in the war, but this is how he appeared when the war began.

that July, but Lee's own prospects for making general rank did not look good. He had aged. Lively in his youth, a Kentuckian who knew him in 1860 noted that his 'grave, cold dignity of bearing and the prudential reserve of his manners rather chilled over-early, or over-much intimacy'.

Events, however, were to overtake him and change his entire career. The year 1860 was a presidential year. The old Whig Party had fallen apart, many of the more liberal Whigs joining the new Republican Party. This year marked its second attempt at the presidency, and its candidate was a western politician and lawyer from Illinois, Abraham Lincoln. The Democratic Party, strongest in the South, controlled the White House going into the election with moderate James Buchanan as President. However its convention could not pick a single candidate. Southern fire-eaters, rejecting Illinois Senator Steven A. Douglas, chose their own candidate, John Breckinridge of Kentucky, so there would be two Democratic Party candidates, splitting the national vote, and a number of moderates, mostly old Whigs, formed their own party with their own candidate, which further widened the split.

As a result, Lincoln won the majority of votes cast and swept the Electoral College votes, which were given by state, as well. Lincoln had spoken out against slavery, not calling for its abolition within states already slave, but stopping it from spreading into western states. Many Southern leaders felt that if slavery could not spread it would eventually die in slave states as well. Moreover, they mistrusted Lincoln's determination to execute laws on the books that called for the return of fugitive slaves. Therefore, Southern hotheads decided to overthrow the results of an election they did not win by popular vote by simply taking their states out of the Union. On 10 December 1860, South Carolina voted to secede from the Union, and other deep-south slave states followed suit.

While such Southern leaders announced to the world that their leaving the Union to form a new nation was based on slavery, Lee had ambivalent feelings about the subject. He had written to his wife on 27 December 1856: 'In this enlightened age, there are few I believe, but what will acknowledge, that slavery as an institution, is a moral & political evil in any Country. It is useless to expatiate on its disadvantages. I think it however a greater evil to the white than to the black race, & while my feelings are strongly enlisted in behalf of the latter, my sympathies are more strong for the former. The blacks are immeasurably better off here than in Africa, morally, socially & physically.'

Lee's home state was not among those that left the union in the first wave of seceded states. Years earlier he had sworn an oath to defend the Constitution of the United States, and he felt a loyalty to his home state. As Episcopalians look for the *via media*, the middle ground, on religious issues, so did he on this political issue. On 14 December he wrote: 'Feeling the aggressions of the North, resenting their denial of the equal rights of our citizens to the common territory of the commonwealth, etc., I am not pleased with the course of the "Cotton states" as they term themselves. In addition to their selfish, dictatorial bearing, the threats they throw out against the "Border States", as they call them, if they will not join them, argue little for the benefit. While I wish to do what is right, I am unwilling to do what is wrong, either at the bidding of the South or the North.' But on 5 December he had written to his son, 'If the Union is dissolved, which God in his mercy forbid, I shall return to you. If not, tell my friends to give me all the promotion they can.' Obviously Lee was considering his options.

On the whole it appears that he determined to go with the South from a fairly early date. He wrote on 22 January 1861: 'I wish to live under no other government, & there is no sacrifice I am not ready to make for the preservation of the union save that of honour. If a disruption takes place, I shall go back in sorrow to my people & share the misery of my native state, & save in her defence there will be one soldier less in the world than now.' He seems to have explained his own motive in a biography of his father he wrote in 1869, when he emphasised a sentence in one of his father's writings: *'No consideration on earth could induce me to act a part, however gratifying to me, which could be construed into disregard or forgetfulness of this Commonwealth* [of Virginia].'

On 1 February 1861 Texas voted to leave the Union and on the 4th Lee was ordered to report to Winfield Scott in Washington. Texas officials offered him a Confederate commission which he refused. He reached Alexandria on 1 March and had a long meeting with Winfield Scott, but what was discussed is not known. He was offered a Confederate brigadier general's commission on the 15th, which he ignored, and the next day was offered a U.S. Army colonel's commission, which he accepted, as of 30 March.

In the meantime, in response to a Southern bombardment of the U.S. Army's Fort Sumter in Charleston Harbour, Lincoln called for volunteers from the various states to put down the insurrection. Virginia's governor refused to supply troops and state leaders met to discuss secession. On 17 April they voted to secede, subject to a popular referendum to be held on 23 May. In the meantime Virginia militia began seizing federal government property.

Lee, fully aware of the Virginia convention being held, met Francis P. Blair, Sr., an adviser to Lincoln, and then Scott on 18 April. While Blair seems to have offered him a chance for Union high command, Scott advised him to resign as quickly as possible if that was his plan. On the 20th he sent a letter of resignation to the War Department. On the 21st Virginia's Executive Council recommended that Lee be nominated commander of all state forces. On the 22nd Lee accepted this commission, although his resignation would not be official until the 25th. On 14 May 1861, Lee was commissioned a brigadier general in the Confederate Army, the highest rank available at the time in that fledgling force, accepting the commission even before Virginia was part of the Confederacy. It would not be until 8 June that Virginia's military forces would be transferred to the Confederacy. Lee was now in the uniform that he would make famous.

SUCCESS AND FAILURES

On 22 April 1861, Lee checked into the Spotswood Hotel in Richmond. The next morning he opened a temporary office and wrote his General Order No. 1, which announced his assumption of the command of Virginia's military forces. As yet he had no staff or even a clerk assigned to him. This would soon change. Colonel Charles Dimmock was appointed to head the state ordnance department, and a full staff that included an adjutant general, a paymaster, a surgeon general, and a quartermaster was appointed on the 25th.

For line troops Lee could call on the state militia which, on paper, consisted of some 200,000 men in four divisions. Many of these units, however, were of little real value, being moribund. Most of them had never actually functioned in their assigned positions. The real defence would fall to the 18,000 members of the state's volunteer militia companies, men who had purchased their own uniforms and trained in their non-working hours. Many were new companies, raised after the John Brown raid. None of these was larger than a company nor did they have any officers of higher rank than captain. There were exceptions: Richmond's 1st Regiment of Virginia Volunteers had been formed in 1851, and was well trained, uniformed and equipped.

Lee's immediate concerns were focused on the U.S. Armoury at Harpers Ferry to the north-west and the Norfolk Navy Yard and Fort Monroe to the south-east. State forces had taken the navy yard, which Federal sailors had largely burned although much of military value was saved. Fort Monroe would remain in Federal hands throughout the war and be a constant threat. Lee sent out orders to muster troops at both locations.

There was an infantry regiment readily available in the west. The 2nd Virginia had been organised in 1860 from volunteer militia companies assigned to the official 55th Virginia, the Jefferson County paper militia regiment. On 18 April the governor ordered this into service at Charles Town from where they were to move into Harpers Ferry. On 1 May he ordered Colonel Thomas J. Jackson, late an instructor at the Virginia Military Institute and now commander of the troops at Harpers Ferry, to call out volunteer companies from Berkeley, Clarke, Frederick, Hampshire, Hardy, Jefferson, and Morgan Counties. Jackson's orders called for him to pick uniformed and armed companies as much as possible and to form them into regiments. He also

Lee as seen by an English artist, whose drawing of him was then published in *Harper's Weekly Magazine*, during the early part of the war. Lee himself described his coat as being grey and his trousers blue.

29

had the arms-making equipment sent from Harpers Ferry to Richmond to be set up there and small-arms production resumed.

Jackson immediately showed his aggressive nature. Although Lee wanted to avoid active fighting as long as possible, Jackson disliked Harpers Ferry, a town surrounded by hills on every side, and planned to take the hills across the Potomac River in Maryland, a state that had not joined the Confederacy. Lee advised against this move, writing on 10 May, 'The true policy is to act on the defensive, & not invite an attack.' Jackson was adamant and went ahead with drawing up plans for an attack.

On the seaboard, Lee sent the state engineer to lay out fortifications supported by artillery. A local unit, the 3rd Virginia, had been in existence there since the mid-1850s and was officially ordered into service for local defence on 20 April. He followed these with more troops, including the first Confederates to arrive in Virginia from Alabama and Georgia. At the same time he had all the unnecessary military equipment brought away from the Norfolk Navy Yard to safer areas, and sent more artillery to the Virginia side of the Potomac River.

A full state mobilisation was ordered on 3 May. That day Lee sent orders to the commanders at Alexandria, Norfolk, and Fredericksburg to call out local volunteer companies and organise them into regiments. Companies from the same general areas were to be kept together as much as possible. Later in the month all the state's volunteer companies were called to the colours to be formed into regiments.

On 10 May Jefferson Davis appointed Lee to command all Confederate troops in Virginia. Less than a week later he nominated Joseph Johnston, who earlier had gone to Montgomery, Alabama, the Confederacy's temporary capital, to meet Davis personally, to command all Virginia forces at Harpers Ferry. Davis neglected to tell Lee of this appointment, Lee only learning of it when Johnston sent him a copy of his orders. Johnston arrived at Harpers Ferry and assumed command, before Jackson could invade Maryland, undoubtedly to Lee's great relief.

Davis himself saw matters in Virginia of such grave consequence that he set out for the state. At the same time, he called for P. G. T. Beauregard, the Confederate commander at the taking of Fort Sumter, to head for Virginia himself. Davis arrived in Richmond on 29 May and Beauregard a day later. On the 30th Davis, Beauregard

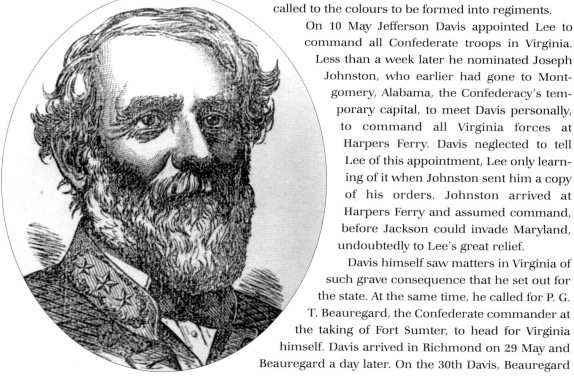

The face of Lee best known to period Southern citizens, as he appeared in the *Southern Illustrated News*. Note the standing collar, which he would change to a more comfortable lay-down style after his heart troubles began in early 1863.

and Lee held a planning session and, as a result, Davis sent Beauregard to command the forces gathered at Manassas.

Now Johnston was Confederate commander in western Virginia and Beauregard in eastern Virginia, with Davis in overall control, working through the Confederate Secretary of War and Adjutant and Inspector-General Samuel Cooper. On 8 June, when Virginia's forces were officially absorbed into those of the Confederacy, Lee's position became unclear. He was a Confederate brigadier general, but apparently lacked a command, writing home the next day that he did not 'know what my position will be. I should like to retire to private life, if I could be with you & the children, but if I can be of any service to the State or her cause, I must continue.'

Without any defined duties, Lee hung around headquarters doing what he could to be helpful as Beauregard and Johnston fought the First Manassas, successfully fending off a Union drive on Richmond. Johnston then remained east and took over command of the army gathered between Richmond and Washington. On 28 July 1861, Davis sent Lee to western Virginia, where Union troops had taken advantage of anti-slavery feelings to capture a part of Virginia. Lee was not given actual overall command there, merely ordered to serve as a 'co-ordinator' between various Southern forces already in the field. As the Richmond *Examiner* put it, Lee's role was to 'be one of inspection, and consultation on the plan of campaign'.

On August 31, Congress confirmed a list of individuals to be promoted to full general, and Lee was third on the list.

The area soon to become a new state, West Virginia, was not a happy place for the Confederates. Richard B. Garnett, one of the state's leading generals, had been sent there earlier and had been killed in a defeat. Davis had nominated two other individuals as generals there, John B. Floyd and Henry A. Wise. Neither had professional military experience but were politicians. Floyd had been U.S. Secretary of War, while Wise had been Virginia's governor; both were old political rivals. A third general in the theatre, William W. Loring, had seen service in the Mexican War, where he lost an arm. None of the three displayed the least bit of military competence and, moreover, feuded with one another. One observer noted that in particular Floyd and Wise were 'as inimical to each other as men can be, and from their course and actions I am fully satisfied that each of them would be highly gratified to see the other annihilated'.

On top of that, Lee found the rank-and-file in poor condition, writing home on 4 August: 'The soldiers everywhere are sick. The measles are prevalent throughout the whole army, & you know that disease leaves unpleasant results, attacks on the lungs, typhoid, &c., &c., especially in camp where accommodation for the sick is poor.' Lee tried to get the generals there to organise their forces, and work together.

Finally he felt able to take the offensive. His target was Cheat Mountain, a high point commanding a major turnpike and several mountain passes, garrisoned by some 2,000 Union troops under Brigadier General Joseph J. Reynolds. Lee personally took command of Loring's force, some 15,000 Confederates, and planned to attack the Federals with some of his troops taking the mountain top, held by one Union regiment, and the rest attacking the turnpike, held by five regiments.

Despite heavy rain, Lee struck on 11 September with skirmishing forces. The rain continued into the next day, when Lee attacked with all his forces. But poor staff work in co-ordinating the attacks led to a total failure. The attack on the mountain top never came off at all, and the Federals held the remainder of their line easily. Intelligence from captured Union soldiers convinced Lee that he was facing a force twice his size. When Reynolds was reinforced, Lee continued to skirmish along the lines on the 13th, but finally had to withdraw his troops. Lee noted that the battle failed because the rain had rendered weapons unusable and the men were 'in poor condition for a fierce assault against artillery & superior numbers', as well as the failure to take the mountain top. Moreover, he expected to win but 'the Ruler of the Universe willed otherwise to send a storm to disconcert a well-laid plan, & to destroy my hopes.'

The Battle of Cheat Mountain was Lee's first command in battle, and it had been a total failure. But it created a pattern that all his battles would thereafter follow. Lee would decide on a bold, aggressive plan. He would give over its actual operation to his staff and subordinate commanders, who might succeed or fail. He would, however, remain on the field, even after a failed attack, until it was quite obvious that there was no way to turn failure into success.

Lee, who had been criticised for his earlier defensive mode on taking command of Virginia's forces, was now heaped with even more criticism for his part in the West Virginia campaign. He was recalled to Richmond, and on 6 November was sent to command the Atlantic coastal defences in South Carolina, Georgia, and northern Florida.

Lee found the troops there split in penny packets in small forts all along the extreme outer limits of the coast lines. Two of these small sea island forts fell just

Lee managed his relationship with Jefferson Davis, never an easy man to get along with, quite well by almost over-informing him of every detail in his army. (Library of Congress)

before Lee arrived in Georgia and it was obvious that the superior Union naval and military power could capture almost any other posts at will.

As Lee wrote to the governor of Florida, when he looked at the entire coast line defence: 'it becomes important to ascertain what points can probably be held, & what points had better be relinquished. The force that the enemy can bring against any position, where he can concentrate his floating batteries, renders it prudent & proper to withdraw from the islands to the main & to prepare to contest his advance into the interior.' Immediately Lee ordered the scattered posts abandoned, concentrating his forces so that they could be rushed to threatened points by coastal railways. He also concentrated on defending the major objectives in the area, Savannah and Charleston. He ordered waterways leading inland to be blocked by obstacles, while designing and overseeing the production of extensive fortifications, especially Fort Pulaski, east of Savannah, and works around Charleston Harbour.

On 8 January 1862, he wrote to General Samuel Cooper, the army's Adjutant and Inspector-General, a post designed to function as a chief of staff, that he hoped 'that when completed, armed, & manned, if properly fought, the enemy's approach ought to be successfully resisted. I am aware that we must fight against great odds, & I always trust that the spirit of our soldiers will be an overmatch to the numbers of our opponents.' This trust in the spirit of the Confederate soldier making his a better fighting machine than the Union enemy's was one that Lee constantly depended on.

In January, too, Lee took advantage of his posting to make his only visit to his father's grave on Cumberland Island, Georgia. Although his occupation gained him the nickname 'The King of Spades', he designed a system of defensive works that was so efficient that neither Charleston nor Savannah fell until the last months of the war. Davis found, however, that he missed Lee's advice and ordered him back to Richmond. On 5 March 1862, Lee left Charleston for Richmond.

There Lee was 'charged with the conduct of military operations in the army of the Confederacy ...' In fact, Davis, who fancied himself a military expert, took his constitutional job of Commander-in-Chief seriously, and in no way would relinquish direct control of military operations. Lee was more commonly referred to as the 'military adviser to the president', although he was rarely asked for advice and functioned in fact as a liaison between army commanders and Davis.

Davis was not an easy person to work with and the high command as a result was in something of a turmoil. The young government was on its third secretary of war; Davis had at best strained relationships with two important field commanders, Beauregard in the west and Johnston in Virginia. In part both generals shared the blame for this state of affairs. Beauregard went behind Davis' back to push for personal glory in the press. Johnston was a very similar man to Davis, proud and unable to admit fault or compromise with another's point of view. He felt that his pre-war U.S. Army position should have made him the Confederacy's senior general and threatened resignation when others were named higher than he on the list of generals. Only soothing talk from comrades prevented this, but neither man got along thereafter. Davis lost his trust in Johnston when the general abandoned his position near Manassas, destroying much precious *matériel* in a needless rush to retire towards Richmond, even though he was not actually under threat.

Union forces, however, were active. Union Army of the Potomac commander Major General George B. McClellan came up with a plan to transport his army to the end of the peninsula that juts into the Chesapeake Bay, controlled by the U.S. Navy. From there he could advance west on to Richmond. The route was shorter and less cut up by rivers than the overland route south from Washington which Lincoln favoured. Lincoln eventually accepted McClellan's plan, and by 4 April the Union army was in position.

Confederates there were under Major General John B. Magruder. An old soldier, Magruder pulled his forces back to lines set up around Yorktown that took advantage of natural waterways. Johnston wanted to concentrate the entire army, which Lee referred to in his correspondence as 'The Army of Northern Virginia', on the peninsula, but Davis insisted on maintaining the defences on both the peninsula and between Richmond and Washington.

McClellan began his move on 15 April, halting in front of Magruder's works. Magruder fooled him into thinking that the Confederate forces were more numerous than was the case, bringing in the same units time and again by train to parade them in front of spying Union eyes. McClellan brought up heavy artillery and began a formal siege. At the same time, Johnston began bringing troops on to the peninsula. But before McClellan could open fire with his heavy mortars, Johnston, against the wishes of Davis and Lee, began withdrawing his men towards Richmond. Union advance forces caught up with retreating Confederates under Major General James Longstreet at Williamsburg on 5 May and fought a fierce fight in heavy rain before the Confederates continued their withdrawal.

The pride of the Confederate Navy, the C.S.S. *Virginia*, often called the *Merrimac* after her original hull, had to be destroyed because she was unable to navigate the shallower waters towards Richmond's navy yard. Federal ships were now able to pass up the James River to Richmond itself. Confederate engineers rapidly built a fort at Drewery's Bluff to prevent this from happening.

Lee was busy all this time serving as a go-between Davis and Johnston as well as other generals in the theatre. But Lee was not the type of man to wait on his opponent before acting. On 17 April he wrote to Major General Richard Ewell, then commanding forces along the Rappahannock, expressing his hope that Ewell could 'strike a successful blow at the enemy in your front … The more active the troops on the Rappahannock, the more on the defensive will the enemy be kept.' His main contribution, however, was co-ordinating commands to support a campaign in the Valley of Virginia to keep the Union forces off balance and so threaten Washington that McClellan would not be reinforced. This campaign would be under the command of Major General Thomas J. ('Stonewall') Jackson.

Jackson suggested such a campaign and Lee, always in favour of aggressive action, instantly approved. Typically for Lee, when Jackson submitted three possible plans, Lee wrote back on 1 May, 'I must leave the selection of the one to be adopted to your judgement.' Jackson's judgement was excellent and the result was his famous Valley Campaign in which he defeated three major Federal forces, cleared the important agricultural area of Federal troops, and seriously concerned Washington officials. Reinforcements did not reach McClellan.

Lee's first corps commander was James Longstreet, whom he called his 'old warhorse'. Longstreet is seen here wearing the first regulation Confederate general's uniform. (Lee-Fendall House)

On the peninsula Lee and Davis both viewed Johnston's continued withdrawal with concern. On 12 May Lee wrote to Johnston, 'As our troops recede the enemy will naturally follow. Toward what point in the vicinity of Richmond do you desire them to concentrate?' Johnston, who continually annoyed Davis by keeping him in the dark about his plans, did not reply. Instead he pulled back the army to the suburbs of Richmond, from where Federals could see the church spires of Richmond. Davis insisted that Johnston, who was giving every sign of being willing to give up Richmond to avoid a fight, either fight or leave his post. On 31 May, a heavy rain having washed away the bridges over the Chickahominy River and thereby separated two Federal corps from the main army, Johnston finally struck.

Poor staff work and verbal, rather than written, orders directing the complicated plan Johnston had concocted, caused Confederate units to get totally confused in the line of march to the battle. Finally units commanded by Major General A. P. Hill, impulsive as he would prove to be thereafter, attacked Union forces near the Seven Pines. While the Federals were holding their lines, despite being outnumbered, against piecemeal Confederate attacks, Davis and his staff arrived on the field. Johnston, perhaps to avoid Davis, rode towards the fighting and was badly wounded.

Command of the army passed to a highly regarded soldier, G. W. Smith. He, however, proved incapable of standing the stress of command, having a nervous breakdown within a day of his assignment. He had to be replaced, and on 1 June 1862 Davis named Lee as the new commander of the Army of Northern Virginia. Lee now found himself in the role that would gain him fame thereafter.

Lee was lucky in the timing. McClellan, never aggressive at the best of times, had been thoroughly shaken by Johnston's attack. He halted his advance, giving Lee time to get acquainted with his new command and make plans for the future. He was not well known in the army, and his reputation as being the 'King of Spades' didn't gain him instant trust with those who had heard of him. J. W. Reid, 4th South Carolina, wrote home after the battle: 'General Johnston is badly wounded. I don't know as yet who will succeed him, but it is said that it will be R. E. Lee, of Virginia. I know but little about him. They say he is a good general, but I doubt his being better than Johnston or Longstreet.'

Artillery officer E. P. Alexander, about two weeks after Lee's assumption of command, noted newspaper articles condemning the choice. He asked a friend on Davis' staff if Lee would have the audacity required for the job. The reply was, 'Alexander, if there is one man in either army, Confederate or Federal, head and shoulders above every other in *audacity*, it is General Lee! His name might be Audacity. He will take more desperate chances and take them quicker than any other general in this country, North or South; and you will live to see it, too.'

Apparently aware of the need to learn about his army, while letting it learn about him, Lee took advantage of the lull personally to reconnoitre the entire front and informally visit virtually every army unit. Longstreet recalled that: 'General Lee was seen almost daily riding over his lines, making suggestions to working-parties and encouraging their efforts to put sand-banks between their persons and the enemy's batteries, and they were beginning to appreciate the value of such adjuncts. Above all, they soon began to look eagerly for his daily rides, his pleasing yet commanding presence, and the energy he displayed in speeding their labours.'

At the same time a plan of attack was developing in Lee's mind. He noted that despite the Seven Pines battle, McClellan had still left a corps separated from the main army by that meandering stream. Lee planned to strike this corps. On 12 June he sent most of his cavalry to reconnoitre that Union flank. In fact, the cavalry, commanded by J. E. B. Stuart, was able to ride around the entire Union army and report that the Union right was indeed vulnerable.

The army would have to be secretly concentrated. With the Valley cleared of the enemy, Lee was free to bring Jackson's men east to join the main army. At the same time, he shifted most of his troops, some 47,000 men in divisions commanded by Longstreet, A. P. Hill, and D. H. Hill to the same side of the creek as the Union corps rested. The rest of the army, some 25,000 men under Magruder and Benjamin Huger, dug in against an attack by McClellan that Lee, knowing McClellan, frankly didn't expect. 'McClellan', he wrote on 10 June, 'will not move out of his entrenchments …'

McClellan had left that corps to co-operate with an attack he expected to be made overland from Washington. Jackson's Valley Campaign had put an end to that hope and McClellan, well aware that it was now uncomfortably exposed, began to withdraw it. On 25 June Union reconnaissance patrols ran into Lee's vanguard, opening the Seven Days' Campaign. Lee planned the main strike for the next day.

The plan called for careful co-ordination between several striking columns that would have to approach from different directions and at different times in order to attack simultaneously. General Order No. 75, the battle plan, was both complicated and vague: 'Genl Jackson will advance on the road leading to Pole Green Church, communicating his march to Genl Branch, who will immediately cross the Chickahominy, and take the road leading to Mechanicsville. As soon as the movements of these columns are discovered, Genl. A. P. Hill will cross the Chickahominy near Meadow Bridge and move direct upon Mechanicsville … The enemy being driven from Mechanicsville, and the passage across the bridge opened, Genl Longstreet with his division and that of Genl D. H. Hill will cross the Chickahominy at or near that point, Genl D. H. Hill moving to the support of Genl Jackson, and Genl Longstreet supporting Genl. A. P. Hill. The four divisions keeping in communication with each other and moving in echelon, on separate roads, if practicable, the left division in advance, with skirmishers and sharp-shooters extending in their front, will sweep down the Chickahominy, and endeavour to drive the enemy from his position above New Bridge, Genl Jackson bearing well to his left, turning Beaver Dam Creek and taking the direction toward Cold Harbor.'

This didn't happen. Maps were incorrect. Units took wrong roads. Lee's small staff of seven inexperienced officers, most of whom had been civilians before the war, was unable to make things work right. Jackson seemed to fall into a trance and never actually arrived on the field that day. Finally, A. P. Hill was unable to wait any longer and attacked. Hill's men were beaten back, while some of D. H. Hill's brigades came up with unco-ordinated attacks that also failed. Confederate losses were some 1,484 with only 364 Union losses.

That night the Federals fell back to Gaines' Mill where they formed a strong semicircular defence. Lee determined to press the attack on the 27th. Day-long attacks failed until dark when Confederates punched a hole in the Union line. All the same, it was too little, too late; the Federals bought a day for McClellan to pre-pare a main defence at great cost to the Confederate army. That night the Federals retreated, as Lee struck again on the 28th and 29th. On the 30th a Union rear guard held off Lee's attacks as the main Union army prepared a heavily protected line based on Malvern Hill, overlooking McClellan's naval base on the James River.

On the 30th Lee prepared to attack again. As he and Longstreet reconnoitred along a flank, D. H. Hill, supported by Jackson, struck Union artillery positions on Malvern Hill. Losses were terrible as the Confederates were beaten off. By now, however, McClellan was in a safe position and Lee knew he could not again attack successfully. The Seven Days' Campaign was over. Lee had lost some 3,300 killed, 16,000 wounded, and 1,000 missing, five thousand more casualties than the Federals received. However, he had thoroughly shaken McClellan to the point where his campaign was over and Richmond was safe. He had been able to evaluate his generals and made quick replacements, having Magruder and Huger sent to other assignments.

With Richmond safe and McClellan penned in, Lee turned his attention north. There Lincoln, despairing of getting McClellan to attack, placed all the assorted units in the Washington area under Major General John Pope. Pope had come from western theatre successes to command this group, styled the Army of Virginia. Immediately Pope published a number of orders, apparently deriding eastern generals as being concerned with ways to retreat. Moreover, he called for drastic measures in Virginia, feeding his troops with confiscated food and destroying houses in areas where guerrillas fired on Union troops. Moreover 'disloyal' Virginians, presumably all white males, were to be arrested and paroled to their homes. If later found to be engaged in prohibited activities, they were to be shot and their property seized.

Lee was horrified by these orders. He sent Jackson and his command north, adding A. P. Hill's division for support and ordering, on 27 July, 'I want Pope to be suppressed. The course indicated in his orders if the newspapers report them correctly cannot be permitted and will lead to retaliation on our part.' On 7 August he sent Jackson a note in which he 'ventured to suggest for your consideration not to attack the enemy's strongpoints, but to turn his position at Warrenton, &c., so as to draw him out of them. I would rather you should have easy fighting and heavy victories.' This type of vague suggestions as to what subordinates were to do was typical of Lee's style, as was the desire for 'heavy victories'.

On 9 August Jackson's lead elements ran into the Union Army of Virginia's II Corps under Major General Nathaniel Banks at Cedar Mountain, south of Culpeper. Unfortunately Hill was not informed of Jackson's movement, although his division was only eight miles away and could have been ordered up for support. The Federals attacked, breaking the famed Stonewall Brigade and turning Jackson's left. Pressing the Confederates back, Jackson's command was only saved when Hill's Light Division arrived on the field towards evening. With this the tables were turned and the Federals forced back, Hill's men in pursuit. It had been a costly and hard-fought victory.

After a brief rest, Jackson put his men on the road again, capturing the Federal railway supply depot at Manassas. There his men looted much needed food before setting what they couldn't carry away on fire. Pope reacted by turning north-west in pursuit of Jackson. But Jackson was like a bee, flitting away and then striking at will against a blind opponent.

Leaving G. W. Smith to command the troops penning in McClellan, Lee himself rode north to join the bulk of the army now concentrating there. He also had Longstreet's command brought up to Jackson's aid and it went into line, unknown to the Federals, on Jackson's right. On 19 August Lee issued Special Order No. 185 that set up an attack on Pope's army. Jackson's command would make up the left wing of the army and move towards Culpeper Court House, while Longstreet's command would move on the right and keep in contact with Jackson.

On the 28th Jackson lured Pope to attack by striking a division at Groveton. Pope acted the next day as Jackson wanted, hurling his men at prepared Confederate positions on the old Manassas battlefield. That evening the Confederates compacted their lines and Pope's scouts, seeing the movement, interpreted it as meaning that the Confederates were retreating. Taking advantage of this perceived retreat, Pope ordered renewed attacks on the morning of the 30th. Again multiple attacks against Jackson's position failed and, as the Union efforts grew frailer, Longstreet struck, rolling up the Union left and smashing Pope's army. Only nightfall and a stubborn defence on Henry House Hill saved the Army of Virginia from annihilation. Pope retreated towards Centreville that evening.

Completely different characters from each other, Lee placed a great deal of trust in his second corps commander, Thomas J. ('Stonewall') Jackson. This image of the great general was made in 1862.

As so often, rain fell after the battle. On 30 August, when reconnoitring near Stewart's farm Lee dismounted to give some orders. As he did so, his horse, Traveller, startled at a nearby commotion began to spring away. Lee made an impulsive grab for the reins, but tripped on his rubberised raincoat. He broke his fall with both hands, suffering a broken bone in one hand and spraining the other. He would not be able to ride or even write personal notes until mid-October.

Lee always sought a total victory. Unwilling to rest, despite his injury, he ordered Jackson's men to go after Pope. In pouring rain, Jackson's weary 'foot cavalry' caught up with the Federal rear guard at Chantilly on 1 September. Several Confederate attacks under A. P. Hill were beaten back and the Army of Virginia continued its successful retreat to the protection of Washington's fortifications.

Lee now proposed a dramatic effort. On 3 September he wrote to Davis that the Army of Northern Virginia 'should enter Maryland'. Not only were the Union forces there in disarray, but Maryland, a slave state, would get a chance 'of throwing off the oppression to which she is now subject ...' Lee admitted that his army had problems: it 'lacks much of the material of war, is feeble in trans-portation, the animals being much reduced, and the men are poorly prepared with clothes, and in thousands of instances are destitute of shoes. Still we cannot afford to be idle ...' Lee never wanted a passive defence, 'to be idle'.

Davis approved Lee's plan, and on 4 September the Army of Northern Virginia's troops began crossing the Potomac River north. They were forced to leave thousands of men who lacked shoes south of the Potomac River, on assignment to temporary commands. By the 7th the entire army was in Maryland, and a day later Lee issued a proclamation offering the aid of his troops to local citizens to 'throw off this foreign yoke ... and restore independence and sovereignty to your State'. In fact, Marylanders, especially in the western part of the state where Lee's men were on the march, had no such desires. Confederates were disappointed to find stores shuttered and locals uninterested in joining the ranks of such tattered troops as themselves. As Walter Taylor, an adjutant on Lee's staff wrote home on 7 September, 'Some seem rejoiced at our advent amongst them; others manifest either indifference or a silence which bespeaks enmity.'

As in the Second Manassas campaign, Lee divided his army, issuing Special Order No. 191 that spelled out how the forces were to form two columns. Jackson's men were to take Harpers Ferry and then march north to join Longstreet's command. In Washington, Pope was quickly relieved of command and sent west to fight Native Americans; McClellan was restored to overall com-mand. He began moving troops westwards towards the reported Confederate position. Unfortunately for Lee, some of McClellan's soldiers found a copy of Lee's Special Order No. 191 wrapped around three cigars. They quickly recog-nised the paper for what it was and it was rapidly sent up the chain of command to McClellan's headquarters where an officer who knew the signature of Lee's staff officer who had signed it saw it was genuine.

Armed with Lee's plans, McClellan first let some sixteen hours slip by, but then began moving rather quickly for him. In the lost time, Lee learned that his orders had been discovered, and sent orders for the nearest troops to defend the gaps in the mountain range that ran north to south and shielded his forces from McClellan's. On 14 September Federal advance forces struck outnumbered Confederates at Fox's Gap and the Boonsborough Gap. Only reinforcements from Longstreet's command prevented a disaster, but the Federals had broken through by the day's end. Other Federal troops attacked Crampton's Gap, but were held successfully. Lee prepared to fall back into Virginia.

On the morning of the 15th Jackson was able to report the capture of Harpers Ferry, and 13,000 small arms and 73 cannon. Lee changed his mind about retreating and concentrated his troops in the small town of Sharpsburg just north of the Potomac River. One ford there would be his only route of escape if worst came to worst.

Leaving a division at Harpers Ferry to deal with prisoners, Jackson force-marched his troops that night and reached Sharpsburg in time. There was, as there had been in the entire campaign, much straggling. Lee complained to Davis on the 13th: 'Our great embarrassment is the reduction of our ranks by straggling, which it seems impossible to prevent with our present regimental officers. Our ranks are very much diminished, I fear from a third to a half of the original numbers …'

Lee drew up lines around Sharpsburg, his right flank resting on high ground that overlooked the Antietam Creek, his centre based on a sunken farm road, and the left flank in fields, woods, and a Dunker church. McClellan slowed down as his forces approached so as to give Lee time to deploy. On the foggy morning of 17 September McClellan began the assault, but piecemeal, first with the right wing and then the centre, both attacks petering out. Lee was able to shift troops

Antietam Bridge, Maryland. Alexander Gardner. (US War Dept.)

ANTIETAM: MORNING ACTION TO 1PM

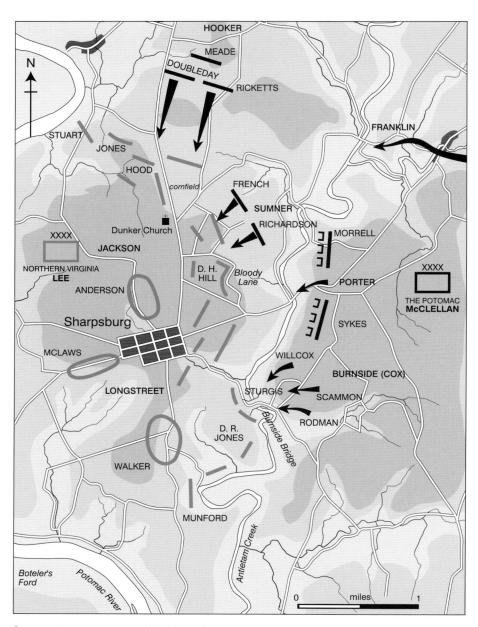

from point to point and hold the line. As the centre attacks faded, the attack on Lee's right, across the Antietam Creek hit home and the Confederate line began to falter. At three in the afternoon it appeared McClellan might win the battle.

At this point, however, advancing troops could be seen. Their flags showed them to be A. P. Hill's Light Division which had forced-marched from Harpers Ferry to reach Sharpsburg just in time. The Federal attack was baulked. McClellan had an entire corps in reserve and could have sent this forward,

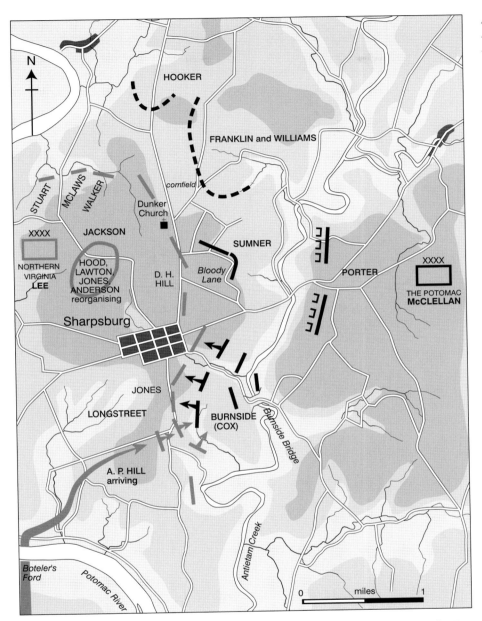

which would probably have meant the end of the Army of Northern Virginia. But his courage failed, and as darkness fell Lee's troops were still in position.

Fighting this battle was Lee's greatest mistake during the war. It was unnecessary. He could have continued to fall back towards Harpers Ferry while skirmishing with McClellan's troops to keep them occupied. From there he could have headed down the Valley of Virginia and swung round to protect Richmond before the slow-moving McClellan could do anything. Or he could have crossed the river and threatened McClellan's left as the Union forces headed towards Harpers Ferry, which surely would have stalled McClellan's advance. Instead he chose to fight, his back to the river, in a position where a more aggressive and able general would have destroyed the major Confederate army in the east. In the process the army suffered almost 14,000 casualties in the bloodiest single day of the war.

It was not enough to stifle Lee's spirit. That night he and Jackson examined the position on their left to determine if an attack there could be successful. They decided it was unlikely. But he kept the army in its lines for an entire day, hoping that McClellan would renew the attack, before finally retreating, unharassed, back into Virginia. For his part McClellan had had enough. He declined to resume the offensive next day, and remained in Maryland for some time to come, rejoicing that the Confederates had been driven off.

Despite this setback, it took a while before Lee abandoned his raid into Maryland. Taylor wrote home on 28 September: 'I believe my Chief was most anxious to recross into Maryland but was persuaded by his principal advisers that the condition of the army did not warrant such a move. This is conjecture on my part. I only know of his opinion & *guess* why he did not follow it. At this time it would have been hazardous to re-enter Maryland. With the men of the army that state now meets but little sympathy.' On a personal note, Lee's daughter Annie died on 20 October aged 23, which was a matter of deep sorrow for the general.

So the army fell back to Martinsburg to refit and rest. McClellan did not follow into Virginia until prodded by Lincoln. On 28 October, two days after McClellan's troops finally crossed the Potomac, Lee moved the army to Culpeper, leaving Jackson in the Valley to block McClellan's move towards Gordonsville. This divided the army into two elements, which he called the Left and Right Wings. Since this essentially created two corps, on 6 November he had Longstreet and Jackson promoted to lieutenant general, a new rank, each in command of a wing.

A day later Lincoln, who had had enough of inaction, removed McClellan from command, replacing him two days later with Major General Ambrose Burnside. Burnside proposed an overland strike directly at Richmond from the Washington area, and Lincoln approved. By 17 November Burnside's advance elements had reached the Rappahannock River, just upriver from Fredericksburg. Lee began to concentrate his troops there, while Burnside concentrated the Army of the Potomac across the river, waiting for pontoon bridges to be sent from Washington.

Lee's lines were actually on the heights above Fredericksburg, the town being built on a hill sloping up from the river. Across the river Federal artillery dominated the town itself, citizens being informed on the 21st that they must surrender or evacuate the town. Most did flee, in a snowstorm, that night and next morning. In the meantime, Lee ordered Jackson to leave a garrison in the Valley and join Longstreet's Right Wing at Fredericksburg, On 1 December Jackson moved into the line on Longstreet's right. While waiting for action to begin, Lee learned of the death of a grandchild, daughter of Fitzhugh Lee.

On 11 December, the bridges finally in place, Burnside's army began crossing the river. Although his planned dash towards Richmond had been thwarted by Lee's deployment, Burnside thought that if his troops could break through to a road running behind and parallel to the Confederate front, he could defeat Lee's army there. On 13 December he ordered his men forward, but it was a forlorn hope. There were minor Union successes on the Confederate right, but the line still held, while the centre of the line above Fredericksburg was not even reached. Union losses were enormous, especially when compared to Lee's.

That cold night Lee considered attacking Burnside's troops, huddled towards the river. To do so, however, would have meant leaving his entrenched positions and crossing the same open field, as the Federals had done earlier, under the direct fire of the Federal artillery that had torn apart the Confederate ranks at Malvern Hill. He decided against the move. Burnside was able to withdraw his army across the river.

Lee put his men into winter quarters in the area, taking advantage of the break in action to reorganise his army's artillery. He reduced the army reserve to six batteries, under Chief of Artillery William Pendleton, an elderly Episcopal priest who had been long out of the military and lacked the respect of many of the younger officers. The other batteries were organised into battalions, each of which would form a corps artillery reserve under a corps artillery commander who would report directly to the corps commander, as well as to Pendleton, although obviously the corps commander would be the more important of the two in action.

Burnside did not give up. On 20 January he set his army marching westwards, along the Rappahannock to cross several fords and turn Lee's flank. Although the weather was fine at first, soon heavy rain began to fall and did so for days. The resulting mud bogged his army down totally. Mules were said to have sunk up to their ears, while artillery pieces sank up to their tubes. Burnside was forced to retire to his old camp. Lee's army was little challenged by this threat, spending most of their time drawing mocking signs such as, 'Burnside stuck in the mud' which they erected ahead of the advancing Federals.

Lee was not only in command of the Army of Northern Virginia, but was also responsible for the defence of the Virginia and North Carolina coast lines. The Federals began making aggressive moves in this area, and Lee sent Longstreet with 16,000 men in divisions commanded by John Bell Hood and George Pickett, as well as a cavalry brigade, south of the James. This detachment was ordered partly because of the Federal threat, but as much because, as he wrote on 5 January 1863, 'Our men & animals have suffered much from scarcity of food & I fear they are destined to more.' Longstreet's detachment would relieve some of the pressure on the local infrastructure. The result of this move, which was not to prove successful in that theatre, was that Lee's army would be minus its senior corps commander and a quarter of its men into the spring of 1863.

He personally began to show the strain of his years. On 9 March 1863, he wrote to his wife, 'Old age & sorrow is wearing me away, & constant anxiety & labour, day & night, leave me but little repose.' On about the 27th he developed what he believed to be a severe sore throat, accompanied with sharp paroxysms of pain in his chest, back and arm, apparently a heart attack. On the 30th he was moved from his headquarters to a private home where he was attended by the army's medical director as well as another surgeon, a noted doctor from New Orleans.

On 3 April he wrote to his wife: 'I am getting better I trust though apparently very slowly & have suffered a great deal since I last wrote. I have had to call upon the doctors who are very kind & attentive & do every thing for me that is possible. I have taken a violent cold, either from going in or coming out of a warm house, perhaps both, which is very difficult to get rid of & very distressing to have.' Two days later he wrote that he 'was threatened the doctors thought with some malady which must be dreadful if it resembles its name, but which I have forgot … I have not been so very sick, though have suffered a great deal of pain in my chest, back, & arms. It came on in paroxysms, was quite sharp … some fever remains, & I am enjoying the sensation of a complete saturation of my system with quinine.' The medical opinion of that time was that the throat infection 'settled' into a pericarditis, or 'inflammation of the heart sac'. Moreover, the doctors felt some of the pain was caused by rheumatism.

By 12 April he was able to write home, 'I am much better, my cough not annoying, pulse declining, & I am free of pain.' Even so, his heart was permanently damaged: Lee would never again be a well man. He was also suffering, during this time, from 'neuralgia in the head' and a dental abscess.

Despite his bout of bad health, he was unable to escape his many responsibilities. Longstreet, bogged down in a siege of Suffolk, requested more troops, which Lee felt unable to send him. As Federal troops closed in on the last remaining strongholds on the Mississippi, Vicksburg and Baton Rouge, pressures grew to detach troops and send them westwards. And on 27 April, Major General Joseph Hooker, the Army of the Potomac's new commander, set his forces in motion against the Army of Northern Virginia and Richmond.

Hooker's plan was essentially the same as Burnside's (which had got bogged down). He would move up the Rappahannock, and turn Lee's flank, while leaving two corps in front of Fredericksburg to threaten that point. Lee, he was sure, would respond and he could trap the Confederates between the two points. On the 29th Hooker had three corps across the river and making for Lee's exposed south-eastern flank at Ely's Ford. At the same time the two corps at Fredericksburg once again crossed the river, apparently planning to attack across the same ground where Burnside had failed earlier. Late on the 29th Lee sent R. H. Anderson's division to meet the troops concentrating on his flank. By the evening of the 30th the Federals had three corps in a heavily wooded area known as the Wilderness, concentrated around an opening there known as Chancellorsville.

Lee could have fallen back, avoiding action with either wing of the Federal attack. Instead he chose to leave a screening force of Major General Jubal Early's division of some 8,000 men, while rushing the rest to support Anderson in the Wilderness. This plan was even bolder than his choosing to stay and fight around Sharpsburg. It paid off. On the morning of 1 May Hooker learned that Lee was advancing to fight, instead of fleeing as reason dictated. He lost his nerve and pulled his troops back to a defensive position in the dense woods around Chancellorsville, away from the open fields where his superior numbers and artillery would have given him a definite advantage.

In reconnoitring along the line, Stuart's cavalry found that Hooker's right flank was not protected by the river and was open to attack. Lee was surprised that Hooker had chosen to fall back, and wondered whether he was setting a trap, but he jumped at the chance of turning Hooker's right and cutting him off from the Rappahannock, and destroying a large part of the Army of the Potomac.

The effects of a 32-pound shell from a gun of the 2nd Massachusetts Heavy Artillery: Confederate caisson and eight horses destroyed. Federicksburg, 3 May 1863. Capt. Andrew J. Russell. (Mathew Brady Collection)

That night he met Jackson and spelled out the plan. Jackson, as audacious if not more so than Lee, quickly agreed, and had his men on the move next morning. Lee, already short of Early's men at Fredericksburg and Longstreet's at Suffolk, divided his army yet again in the face of a numerically superior enemy. Although Jackson's march was intended to be clandestine, it was noticed at several points by front-line Union troops. In the case of the Union XI Corps, the corps holding the right, warnings were simply ignored. The optimistic Union high command assumed that Jackson was in fact retreating.

It took hours to get into position, although Federal forces did not interfere with Jackson's moves. Towards dusk Jackson finally struck, routing the XI Corps totally. Although elements of the Union army were indeed cut off, most of the army managed to form new defensive lines and hold the Confederate attack as night fell. In the darkness, Jackson and several staff members reconnoitred the front, at one point riding between two front-line North Carolina units. Believing the mounted men to be Union cavalry, one of the regiments fired into the group, killing one of Jackson's engineer officers and wounding Jackson in the hand and arm.

Jackson was carried off the field, the command going to A. P. Hill. He, apparently, was struck by a shell fragment shortly afterwards and was temporarily paralysed. Command passed to Stuart. Lee was woken at 2.30 a.m., on the 3rd with news of Jackson's wounding, and returned to the battle front at daylight. The Confederates continued to attack, but the Federal forces, although cut off, were able to regain their lines and the entire command was able to get back safely across the Rappahannock.

At the Fredericksburg front Early was forced back towards Lee's main position, but when the Federals learned of their loss at Chancellorsville, they, too, turned towards the Rappahannock, which they crossed safely. Lee had had a magnificent victory, but had failed in his real objective, to destroy all or a large part of the Army of the Potomac. Moreover, his force lost 20 per cent of its front-line infantrymen, a total loss of some 10,000 casualties. The most serious loss was that of Jackson who died on 10 May. Lee was deeply shaken by the loss of this officer whom he had grown to depend on greatly: 'Any victory is dear at such a price,' he wrote to his son Custis.

Lee, now facing the major problem of a replacement, came to the conclusion that Jackson's job was simply too big for any single general. 'I have for the past year felt that the corps of this army were too large for one commander ... Each corps contains when in fighting condition about 30,000 men. These are more than one man can properly handle & keep under his eye in battle in the country we have to operate in,' he wrote to Davis on 20 May. He proposed, and Davis agreed, to divide the army into three corps. Longstreet would retain command of a smaller First Corps, A. P. Hill, whom Lee described as 'the best soldier of his grade with me', would have a Third Corps, and Richard Ewell, whom Lee called 'an honest, brave soldier, who has always done his duty well', the Second. Each corps would comprise two divisions.

Moreover, Hooker's defeat in the east did not lessen the main problem confronting the Confederacy, the potential split into east and west by the imminent capture of Vicksburg and Baton Rouge on the Mississippi. Johnston and Beauregard, by now commanding in the western theatre, looked at Lee's army longingly for reinforcements. At this juncture Davis reckoned that Lee could easily defend Richmond, especially after such a victory at Chancellorsville where the army was minus Longstreet's entire corps. Lee, however, believed strongly that his army could not spare a single man, especially after the Maryland Campaign and Chancellorsville, which had been costly in terms of manpower. On 10 June he wrote to Davis: 'We should not therefore conceal from ourselves that our resources in men are constantly diminishing, and the disproportion in this respect between us and our enemies, if they continue united in their efforts to subjugate us, is steadily augmenting. The decrease of the aggregate of this army as disclosed by the returns affords an illustration of this fact. Its effective strength varies from time to time, but the falling off in its aggregate shows that its ranks are growing weaker and that its losses are not supplied by recruits.' On 10 May he had written to Secretary of War James Seddon: 'We are greatly outnumbered by the enemy now … You can therefore see the odds against us and decide whether the line of Virginia is more in danger than the line of Mississippi … [On top of that] I think troops ordered from Virginia to the Mississippi at this season would be greatly endangered by the climate.'

In fact, despite these losses, Lee was playing somewhat fast and loose with the truth. A system of conscription and camps of instruction that forwarded fairly well-trained recruits to front-line regiments, coupled with an excellent hospital system in Richmond that returned a high proportion of wounded and ill to their units, meant that the Army of Northern Virginia actually remained at relatively similar strengths with its enemy throughout the war. The army's aggregate present figures for 31 December 1861 were 76,331; for 30 June 1863, 88,735; for 31 December 1863, 53,995; for 31 December 1864, 71,854; and just before the Appomattox Campaign, 73,349. While it is true that his enemy outnumbered him, they had done so consistently before and would thereafter in relatively the same proportion.

Instead of detaching men from the Army of Northern Virginia to send to the west, Lee argued that if he took the entire army north, into Pennsylvania, he would force the Federal authorities to weaken their forces attacking along the Mississippi. Such a move would also reduce one of Lee's most pressing problems, that of keeping his army fed. Although there was food elsewhere in the Confederacy, the increasingly poor condition of the railways, the wear and tear on wagons, and a general falling apart of the area's infrastructure, meant that it was difficult to get it to Lee's troops.

There was some opposition to his plan, especially from Postmaster General John Regan of Texas, but Lee convinced the president over the course of several meetings in Richmond, although Davis's agreement, at best, was somewhat half-hearted. He felt that the Confederacy should stick to a less costly defence in overall strategic terms. However, his distrust of Johnston's ability to use his troops well, as shown in the Peninsula Campaign, coupled with a belief in Lee's abilities to get the most out of what he had swung him behind the proposal.

South of the James River, on the return of Longstreet's Corps, the remaining troops came under command of D. H. Hill. Lee had had problems with Hill during the Seven Days Campaign, and was not overly fond of the admittedly prickly individual. He tapped Hill's command for additional reinforcements, but Hill baulked at this. Lee, in poor health and greatly concerned with his Pennsylvania plans, dashed off a telegraph to Davis on 29 May that would prove to be a major error in the long run: 'I cannot operate in this manner. I request you to cause such orders to be given him as your judgement dictates.' A day later, still steaming, he wrote Davis a 'request to be relieved from any control of the department from the James to the Cape Fear River.' Davis accepted this, and from now on defence of Richmond from the south would fall to another commander.

The Hill problem settled, on 3 June Lee set his army in motion, moving west where geography would serve to protect his army heading towards Maryland. Stuart's cavalry was left to screen the infantry. The advance went well. Each corps moved separately, with Ewell's in the lead. Ewell quickly captured a major Union garrison at Winchester, in the Valley of Virginia, on 15 June and crossed into Maryland. There the entire army met at Hagerstown, and on the 27th reached Chambersburg, Pennsylvania.

Hooker finally realised that Lee was on the move north, and moved in a parallel line, keeping between the Confederates and Washington. He wanted to abandon Harpers Ferry, but higher command forbade this, whereupon he tendered his resignation, hoping to force them to give him what he wanted. Instead, Lincoln accepted his resignation and named a Pennsylvanian, George Gordon Meade, to command the Army of the Potomac in his place. Meade continued the march north.

But Lee was unaware of what exactly Meade was doing. Stuart had loosely interpreted his orders as giving him a chance to get his name in the papers again by riding

Lee trusted the intelligence provided by his cavalry corps commander, James Ewell Brown (Jeb) Stuart, who would fail him badly, however, in the Gettysburg Campaign.

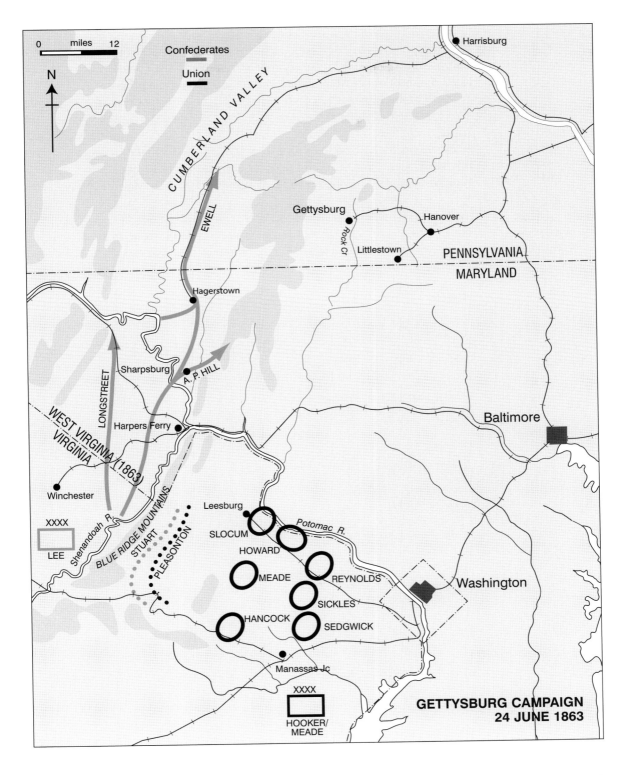

0 miles 12

N

Confederates
Union

CUMBERLAND VALLEY

Harrisburg

EWELL

Gettysburg

Hanover

Rock Cr

Littlestown

PENNSYLVANIA

MARYLAND

Hagerstown

A. P. HILL

Sharpsburg

LONGSTREET

Harpers Ferry

Baltimore

WEST VIRGINIA
VIRGINIA (1863)

Winchester

XXXX

LEE

Shenandoah R.

BLUE RIDGE MOUNTAINS

STUART

PLEASONTON

Leesburg

Potomac R.

SLOCUM

HOWARD

MEADE

REYNOLDS

SICKLES

HANCOCK

SEDGWICK

Washington

Manassas Jc

XXXX

HOOKER/
MEADE

**GETTYSBURG CAMPAIGN
24 JUNE 1863**

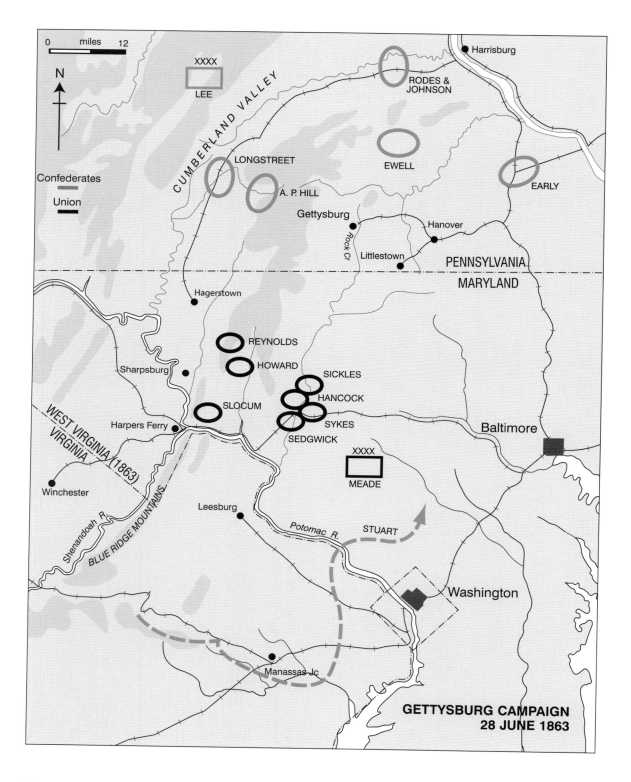

0 miles 12

N

Confederates

Union

XXXX
LEE

CUMBERLAND VALLEY

Harrisburg

RODES &
JOHNSON

LONGSTREET

EWELL

A. P. HILL

EARLY

Gettysburg

Hanover

Rock Cr

Littlestown

PENNSYLVANIA

MARYLAND

Hagerstown

REYNOLDS

HOWARD

Sharpsburg

SICKLES

HANCOCK

SLOCUM

WEST VIRGINIA (1863)

VIRGINIA

Harpers Ferry

SYKES

SEDGWICK

Baltimore

XXXX
MEADE

Winchester

Leesburg

Shenandoah R.

BLUE RIDGE MOUNTAINS

Potomac R.

STUART

Washington

Manassas Jc.

**GETTYSBURG CAMPAIGN
28 JUNE 1863**

entirely around the Union army as he had done so dramatically in 1862. In the process, he captured a long Union wagon train, which he insisted on bringing with him, which slowed his progress. He also ran into Union cavalry at points, such as at Hanover, and this foiled his efforts to reach Ewell's infantry. In short, Stuart's cavalry, so depended on by Lee for intelligence, had gone off the radar screen. He had failed to obey Lee's orders of 23 June to 'move on and feel the right of Ewell's troops, collecting information'.

Lee's army, operating essentially as three independent bodies, made quick progress. By the end of June elements had penetrated as far as the western side of the Susquehanna opposite Harrisburg, the state capital, in the north and Columbia in Lancaster County in the south. Union forces were closing in, and a spy unofficially paid by Longstreet brought word of this to Longstreet who immediately passed the information to Lee. On 28 June Lee ordered his corps commanders to concentrate their forces around Cashtown, just west of Gettysburg, a cross-roads town not far from the Maryland line.

Hill's Corps reached Cashtown, with a brigade going on towards Gettysburg. Although it had been earlier stripped of supplies by Ewell's men on their way towards York, Hill determined to see if more supplies could be found in the town. On 1 July two divisions moved towards the town. On the outskirts they were met by Federal cavalry. Deploying into line and advancing, they pushed the cavalry back. At the same time, the Union cavalry commander got word back to the Union I Corps and its infantrymen marched on, soon reaching the town. Despite Lee's not wanting to engage in a full battle at the very least until all his troops, especially Stuart's wayward cavalrymen, were on the field, this is precisely what was happening.

Lee, however, saw the prospect of victory as Hill's infantry pushed the cavalry and then the infantry back towards the town. He authorised the reinforcement of the fight. Union reinforcements in the form of the XI Corps also dashed on to the field. Determined, if unco-ordinated, Confederate attacks pushed the Union forces back through the town. There they set up a line of defences based on the town's cemetery in somewhat of a U-shape conforming to higher ground. As evening fell, Ewell was strongly pressed by his subordinates to attack and take this ground, but, knowing how worn the troops were from the day's fighting and wanting to wait until fresh troops could take the field, he declined.

That night reinforcements arrived for both sides. The Union line, under direct supervision from Meade who had arrived on the field, took up a defensive line in a fishhook form from Culp's Hill and Spangler's Spring on the right, around the cemetery, and south along Cemetery Ridge to the two Round Tops. The Confederate line conformed to the Union line.

Now Lee's management style began to cause problems. Longstreet had been against the Pennsylvania Campaign from the beginning, writing not long after the war (only one of three of his written accounts that differ in many ways) that he thought 'this movement would be too hazardous …' On the evening of 1 July he met Lee and 'he said, to my surprise, that he thought of attacking General

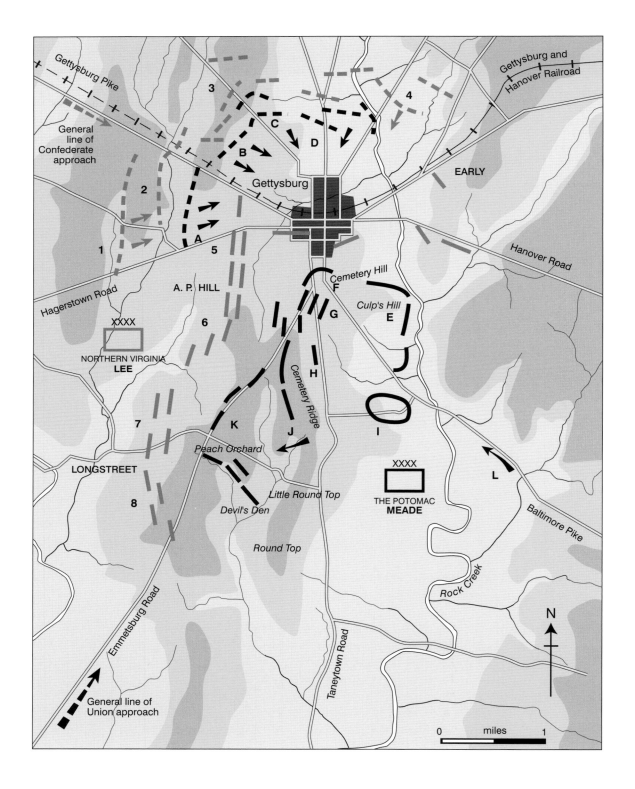

General
line of
Confederate
approach

Gettysburg Pike

Gettysburg and
Hanover Railroad

3

C

D

B

4

EARLY

Gettysburg

2

A

1

5

Hagerstown Road

A. P. HILL

Cemetery Hill

F

G

Culp's Hill

E

6

Hanover Road

XXXX

NORTHERN VIRGINIA
LEE

H

I

Cemetery Ridge

7

K

J

Peach Orchard

XXXX

THE POTOMAC
MEADE

L

LONGSTREET

Little Round Top

8

Devil's Den

Baltimore Pike

Round Top

Rock Creek

Emmetsburg Road

Taneytown Road

N

General line of
Union approach

0   miles   1

GETTYSBURG, 2 JULY 1863

Confederates
Approach to 2.30 p.m.
1 July:
1 Pender
2 Heth
3 Rodes
4 Early

Situation 3.30 p.m.
2 July:
5 Pender
6 Anderson
7 McLaws
8 Hood

Union
Initial forward
deployment:
A Rowley
B Wadsworth
C Robinson
D Schurz

Situation 3.30 p.m.
2 July:
E Slocum
F Howard
G Newton
H Hancock
I Sykes
J Barnes
K Sickles
L Sedgwick

Meade upon the heights the next day'. Longstreet argued for a defensive battle, but, although Lee again said he was determined that Longstreet should attack on 2 July, apparently he failed to do so with a direct order since Longstreet claimed that: 'When I left General Lee on the night of the 1st, I believed that he had made up his mind to attack, but was confident that he had not yet determined as to when the attack would be made.'

In fact, Lee planned attacks on both flanks, with Ewell driving in on Culp's Hill on the left and Longstreet attacking *en echelon*, beginning with Little Round Top and then rolling up the Union line towards its centre. Longstreet, instead, wanted to move around the Big Round Top and then take up a defensive position south of Meade, forcing him to attack in a repeat of Fredericksburg.

The next morning no sounds of Longstreet's attack could be heard. After waiting for a short time to hear of the attack on the right, Ewell went on the attack by himself. This largely failed, although some small gains of ground were made. Lee rode over to find out what happened to Longstreet's attack, only to find none was being made. He told Longstreet that, as Longstreet wrote, 'I should make the main attack on the extreme right.' It was by now 11 a.m.. Unhappy with this decision, Longstreet put his troops on the move. J. B. Hood, one of his divisional commanders, also wanted to move further around past Big Round Top, but an irritable Longstreet told him that this had been forbidden by Lee and he should simply go ahead with the attack.

Longstreet's men finally made the attack, after being forced to make a detour on the line of march to avoid being seen by Union signalmen. After a fierce and bloody exchange, they took Devil's Den and seriously pressed the Federals on Little Round Top. In the end, however, the Union men held the line. In the centre, where the rest of Longstreet's men were to attack *en echelon*, a Federal corps commander foolishly advanced his corps out of line to what he saw as better ground. Longstreet's attack hit there and drove them back in more fierce fighting to their original position. At the end of the day, however, the Union forces held all along the line.

The next time Lee and Longstreet met Lee said he felt that the Union line was much battered and one more push would break through. He wanted Longstreet to attack the Union centre on 3 July. The two argued, but Lee insisted and Longstreet sullenly organised the attack to go into history as Pickett's Charge.

Lieutenant-Colonel Arthur Fremantle, of the British Army's Coldstream Guards, saw him meet the defeated troops coming back from Pickett's Charge: 'If Longstreet's conduct was admirable, that of General Lee was perfectly sublime. He was engaged in rallying and in encouraging the broken troops, and was riding about a little in front of the wood, quite alone – the whole of his staff being engaged in a similar manner further to the rear. His face, which is always placid and cheerful, did not show signs of the slightest disappointment, care, or annoyance; and he was addressing to every soldier he met a few words of encouragement, such as "All this will come right in the end; we'll talk it over afterwards; but, in the meantime, all good men must rally."'

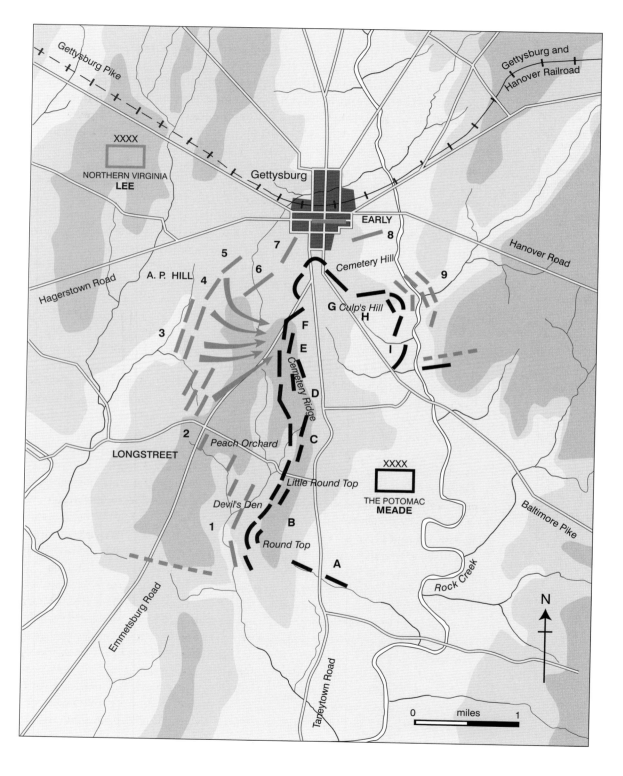

GETTYSBURG, 3 JULY 1863

Union
A Sedgwick
B Sykes
C Sickles
D Doubleday
E Gibbon
F Robinson
G Howard
H Wadsworth
I Slocum

Confederates
1 Hood
2 McLaws
3 Pickett
4 Davis
5 Heth
6 Pender
7 Rodes
8 Early
9 Johnson

In Pickett's charge, as in earlier fighting, Lee failed directly to oversee attack preparations, which was serious given that he was well aware that Longstreet was dead set against the attack. Furthermore, William Pendleton, his artillery chief, failed to co-ordinate maximum artillery support from the corps. Of course, given his recent medical history, one must question Lee's condition during the campaign. Longstreet later wrote that 'Lee suffered during the campaign from his old trouble, sciatica ...' One of Stuart's staff officers, W. W. Blackford, recalled being sent to his headquarters during the battle, and being surprised to 'see him come out of his tent hurriedly and go the rear several times while I was there, and he walked so much as if he was weak and in pain that I asked one of the gentlemen present what was the matter with him, and he told me General Lee was suffering a good deal from an attack of diarrhoea.' No other observers mentioned this, perhaps out of Victorian discretion. At any rate, nothing would seem to have posed such a problem that he was incapable of command.

The next day Lee held his army in its lines, hoping that Meade would counter-attack. But Meade, new to his job and as yet unacquainted with his entire command, held his position as Lee had done after Seven Pines. In pouring rain on 6 July, Lee began his army's retreat, leaving thousands of badly wounded Confederates in hospitals in the Gettysburg area.

Those immediately around Lee did not consider Gettysburg a defeat. After all, they had prevailed largely on the first two days, and the mission of freeing Virginia from fighting so that farmers could work their fields, if only for several weeks, had been successful. Northern civilians had had a lesson at first-hand about the reality of warfare, and Meade's army did not try to counter-attack on 4 July. Lower ranking soldiers and most Southern civilians, however, only saw Lee's troops retiring back to Virginia and, counting the losses, indeed felt it was a defeat. Southern morale fell with this defeat and the capture of Vicksburg on 4 July.

Lee himself wrote to Davis on 8 July, assuring him that, 'I am not in the least discouraged, or that my faith of an all merciful Providence, or in the fortitude of this army, is at all shaken.' Newspaper accounts critical of the army's leadership in the campaign began to appear. Back in Virginia on the 31st, Lee wrote to Davis: 'No blame can be attached to the army for its failure ... I am alone to blame, in perhaps expecting too much of its prowess & valour.' Finally, on 8 August, he wrote to Davis offering to resign, citing both the mounting criticisms and 'the growing failure of my bodily strength. I have not yet recovered from the attack I experienced the past spring. I am becoming more and more incapable of exertion, and am thus prevented from making the personal examinations and giving the personal supervision to the operations which I feel to be necessary ... Everything, therefore, points to the advantages to be derived from a new commander ...' Davis rejected the offer; Lee was clearly the best available commander for the army.

More bad news arrived for Davis. In Tennessee the Federals were driving towards Chattanooga, and Knoxville fell on 30 September. No longer was there a direct railway line between Virginia and the Tennessee theatre. Federal naval and land forces were also pressing the defences of Charleston, South Carolina. In August Davis had Lee come to Richmond for a series of meetings about the overall situation. Lee, who left Longstreet in overall command, wanted badly to get back to the army, but Davis trusted him as he did no other military man and would not allow him to leave.

While there Lee became ill with what he described as 'a heavy cold taken in the hot & badly ventilated rooms in the various departments which resulted in an attack of rheumatism in my back, which has given me great pain & anxiety'. In fact, these appear to have been symptoms of angina pectoris, a temporary decrease in the supply of blood to the heart. He was unable to ride horseback for some time and had to be transported in an army ambulance. By 11 October, when he arrived in Culpeper from Richmond, pains in his back had eased somewhat, but every motion caused him pain.

Davis saw the situation in Tennessee as being very serious, and wanted Lee to go there to assume command from Braxton Bragg, an officer much detested by his subordinates. Lee really didn't want to do this; he wanted to stay where he was. He did, however, agree to send Longstreet's Corps to the Army of Tennessee after Knoxville fell, and some of Pickett's brigades to Charleston, which happened in early September.

Despite his illness, Lee's aggressive nature had not diminished. Learning that the Army of the Potomac had sent two corps to reinforce their forces in Tennessee, he tried the tactic that had worked against Pope in 1862. Meade, however, was not to be trapped in the same way, and fell back towards Centreville, avoiding a major battle. A. P. Hill caught up with his rear-guard at Bristoe Station on 14 October, and launched an attack without adequate reconnaissance or preparation. His men were slaughtered without major losses to the Federals. The next day, after an easy Federal withdrawal, Lee and Hill rode over the field covered with dead Confederates. Lee was obviously displeased as Hill attempted to explain himself. Finally Lee, never one to condemn an officer for overly aggressive behaviour, said to Hill, 'Well General, bury your dead and let us say no more about it.'

While Lee had been technically successful in pushing the Federals back, he now found the army in a land that had been laid waste by several years of soldiers' plundering. Walter Taylor wrote home that the land there was 'desolation made desolate indeed'. Lee wanted to continue pushing Meade back to the Potomac itself, but, as he wrote to his wife, thousands of his troops were 'barefooted, thousands with fragments of shoes, & all without overcoats, blankets or warm clothing. I could not bear to expose them to certain suffering, on an uncertain issue.' And, as he wrote on 28 October, 'My rheumatism is better, though I still suffer.'

Unable to support the army where he was, Lee fell back to the upper Rappahannock, destroying much of the Orange & Alexandria Railroad as he withdrew. Meade followed with the Army of the Potomac, crossing the Rappahannock on 7 November at Kelly's Ford, capturing some 1,200 men and four cannon while suffering only minor losses. Lee was forced to fall back towards Orange Court House, across the upper Rapidan. On 26 November Meade sent forces towards the Chancellorsville area, over the Ely and Germanna Fords. Lee quickly drew up entrenched lines on Mine Run, which ran south from the Rapidan. Taylor wrote home on 5 December 5 that Lee 'gave his attention to the whole line, directing important changes here and there, endeavouring to impress the officers with the importance of success in the impending engagement and presenting a fine example of untiring energy and zest'. His earlier pains seem to have largely been eased.

During the course of 29–30 November Meade's men built works opposite Lee's and planned an assault. The commanders in the front line, however, called off the attack, feeling that it would have been unsuccessful and costly. Meade agreed, and withdrew just before two divisions of Lee's troops struck at what had been the Union left flank but which had now gone. 'I am greatly disappointed at his getting off with so little damage,' he wrote home on 4 December. The weather by now was terrible, biting cold, and both armies went into winter quarters without a major battle having been fought.

The army now in camp, Lee, to whom Davis wrote, 'I need your counsel,' went to Richmond for another series of strategy meetings on the 9th. These would last until 21 December. Davis suggested sending Lee west personally to command the troubled Army of Tennessee. Lee had no wish to leave a command that he had made almost a personal force, however, and suggested that Beauregard would be suited for that command. Davis

This classic image of Robert E. Lee has even appeared on 20th century U.S. postage stamps – probably a unique example of a government allowing the face of a general who tried to destroy it to appear on a nation's stamps. (Library of Congress)

instead picked Joseph Johnston. On his return to the army, Lee ordered some organisational changes, and then returned to Richmond on 22 February. There he found the disgraced Army of Tennessee commander Braxton Bragg recalled to serve as Davis' new military adviser, but Davis continued to depend on Lee's ideas, and in March and April Lee submitted several letters to him outlining potential strategic moves for the 1864 campaign to the president.

After Jackson's death, the divisional commander A. P. Hill, always an informal and colourful dresser, was raised to corps command, but he proved to be less skilful in his new role. (Library of Congress)

Lee noted that U. S. Grant, the victorious general from the west, had been given overall command of all U.S. armies and he had chosen to come east to make his headquarters with the Army of the Potomac. This suggested to Lee that the major Federal push in 1864 would be in the east. Therefore he suggested calling Beauregard from Charleston to command a defence of Petersburg, south of Richmond. He also managed to get Longstreet's Corps, which had failed to capture Knoxville, returned to the Army of Northern Virginia. The corps was marked by its low morale, not only from its defeat, but the quarrelling that had ensued among its commanders. Longstreet proved incapable of independent command.

Grant planned a two-prong attack on Richmond. A political, inept general, Benjamin Butler, landed south of the city to attack northward, towards Petersburg, while Grant with the main Army of the Potomac took the old route south from Washington. Lee had earlier given up command of the south of Richmond, so was not directly concerned with that front, although he lost some troops to the patchwork defence assembled there.

Grant moved south on 3 May, crossing the Rappahannock and entering the Wilderness area, near Chancellorsville. He had hoped to pass quickly through the thick underbrush and into the open before Lee could react, but Lee was ready for him. Lee had planned to strike Grant's column in the heavily wooded area where superior Union numbers, artillery, and cavalry would not count for as much as it would in the open. On the 5th Union troops spotted Lee's lead troops under Ewell, approaching on the Old Turnpike, and Grant ordered an immediate attack. The Confederates were rocked, but reinforcements arrived, and Lee's line held.

Meanwhile, Hill's Corps moved on the Plank Road where it was able to withstand piecemeal attacks from different Union corps. Because of the jungle-like area, where a battalion could leave a road and be entirely invisible within four yards, Lee found himself more on the front line than ever before. He, Hill, and William Pendleton, met Jeb Stuart near a big tree in a small clearing when suddenly Federal infantrymen burst into the clearing. Lee was forced to flee toward the Plank Road.

The next day, Lee planned to counter-attack the Union left flank with units of Longstreet's Corps. Before this could happen, the Federals again attacked Hill's weary men. Hill's two divisions were forced to retreat as Longstreet's men arrived on the field and saved the day. As before, Lee was everywhere on the front line.

Brigadier General Samuel McGowan's South Carolina Brigade was one of those pushed back by the Union advance. Lee rode among them, at one point rebuking the file closers of the 1st South Carolina before meeting McGowan himself. 'My God! General McGowan, is this splendid brigade of yours fleeing like wild geese,' he demanded. An irate McGowan replied, 'Sir, my men are not beaten; they only want a place to reform and fight.' The men themselves, recognising Lee on his famous horse Traveller, stopped and formed a semblance of a battle line and began entrenching.

As Longstreet's troops arrived, Lee rode with them to the front line, at one point being between the 1st Texas and 3rd Arkansas. Again the men recognised him, crying, 'Go back, General Lee. Go back!' Several men grabbed Traveller's reins and turned him back behind the line. Lee then rode over to the brigade commander, John Gregg, calling out, 'General, what brigade is this?'

'The Texas Brigade,' was the reply. As 4th Texas Quartermaster Sergeant John Polley recalled, Lee replied, 'The Texas Brigade always has driven the enemy, and I want them to do it now. Tell them, general, that they will fight to-day under my eye – I will watch their conduct. I want every man of them to know I am here with them!' Gregg rode out in front of us, and told us what General Lee had said, and then gave the command, "Forward!" The word had barely passed his lips when General Lee himself came in front of us, as if intending to lead us. The men shouted to him to come back, that they would not budge an inch unless he did so, and to emphasise the demand, twenty or more of them sprang forward and made an effort to lead or push his horse to the rear … Exactly what occurred, not even those nearest Lee can tell, but just as they got "Traveller" headed to the rear, General Longstreet rode up and said something, whereupon General Lee rode silently back through our ranks.'

Lee now explained to the commander of Humphrey's Mississippi Brigade where and how to deploy, and sent a staff officer to reconnoitre south of the Plank Road. Hardly had he done so when he became aware of Confederate infantry there. 'What troops are these?' he called to one of the officers in the lead. 'Law's Alabama Brigade,' was the reply. 'God bless the Alabamians,' he shouted.

In what became a soldier's battle, Lee was reduced to being as much a cheer-leader as an overall commander. And he performed that function beautifully.

In the meantime, Longstreet had sent his chief of staff to command a force to move around the Union left. The successful attack opened the Plank Road for a general advance. But success was paid for. Longstreet and his staff, as Jackson a year earlier in the same area, were mistaken for Union cavalry. Confederate infantrymen fired into the group, badly wounding Longstreet, who was taken from the field. He would survive, but it would be a long time before he could return to his command.

Grant's army had been badly bloodied, and held to a standstill, but Grant was not of the same stuff as earlier Union generals. Instead of falling back, he ordered his troops to move to the left, to continue south on May 7, heading for Spotsylvania Court House, where he would come between Lee's army and Richmond. Lee quickly realised Grant's plan and, having assigned Robert Anderson to command Longstreet's Corps, ordered that unit to get to Spotsylvania first. The new 1st Regiment of Engineers, a unit whose formation Lee had opposed, built a road through the brush, while cavalry skirmished ahead of the advancing Union forces to slow them down. Anderson's men reached the cross-roads first.

By now both forces had learned to entrench once they reached a line, and when the Federals arrived, they found Confederates dug in across their path. On the 8th Lee ordered Ewell's Corps to reinforce Anderson. As more and more Confederates arrived, the entrenchments soon began to resemble an organised field fortification. Grant, nevertheless, determined to attack, and on the night of 11 May launched his II Corps on the attack. The point selected was a bulge in the Confederate lines, known as the Mule Shoe, and its front was rapidly breached. Lee took personal charge of the defence, ordering in brigades without regard to chains of command. Brigadier General Cullen Battle, commander of an Alabama brigade, later recalled that as his brigade 'passed General Lee on its way to the Bloody Angle, he saluted and stood uncovered until the brigade had passed. I then thought it was a compliment to the Alabama brigade. I now believe he saluted all his soldiers going to the front in the same way.'

Lee got a new line drawn up along the base of the Mule Shoe, from where his men repelled a second attack. Grant's men then dug in while his army received replacements for the heavy losses it had taken so far. Lee, too, received reinforce-ments, in the form of Pickett's division and Hoke's brigade, which were available after Butler's Army of the James allowed itself to be bottled up at the Bermuda Hundred below Richmond. He also received troops that had been earlier serving in the Valley of Virginia and at Hanover Junction. But Lee lost an important commander, Jeb Stuart, killed in a cavalry skirmish during the fighting around Spotsylvania.

Now reinforced, on 21 May Grant again slipped across Lee's front to the south, using his naval base at Port Royal and then swinging back to the Telegraph Road to Richmond. Lee again anticipated the move, and got his troops into position at the North Anna River to block Grant's men. Grant chose to cross several corps at Jericho Mills on the 24th, thereby dividing his army. Lee badly wanted to take advantage of this lapse, but he was suddenly hit with a violent, debilitating bout of an intestinal illness, diarrhoea. He was unable to supervise personally any attack, and was indeed confined to his tent on 25 May. Taylor wrote home on 1 June, 'Since the General's indisposition he has remained more quiet & directs movements from a distance.' In the meantime, Grant realised his potential problem, and withdrew his troops safely across the river.

Grant knew that he couldn't attack Lee's position and on the 26th he again moved to his left, to the south-west, along the north bank of the North Anna towards the Old Church Road that entered Richmond via Mechanicsville. His target was Cold Harbor, which Federal cavalry captured before the infantry could come up. Lee determined to recapture Cold Harbor and ordered infantry to take it, but lacking his personal supervision, the poorly co-ordinated attacks failed. Nevertheless the Confederate infantry held lines around Cold Harbor in well-entrenched positions. Grant determined to make a frontal attack on these lines in the early dawn hours of 3 June. It was his worst mistake of the war and cost his army dearly.

The two weary armies rested thereafter in their lines. Lee took advantage of the lull to send his II Corps, under command of Jubal Early, who had replaced an ailing Richard Ewell, to the Valley to clear it and then threaten Washington. This might, he hoped, so worry the Federal high command that, as they had done before, they would recall all or at least part of the Army of the Potomac to the city's defence.

Grant, who was rarely bothered about his enemy's moves, looked at his maps and determined to swing south again, past Richmond, and take Petersburg. Essentially this would bring Butler's army into better use and place him in a position to take Richmond from its weaker side. On the evening of 12 June he started his army moving south. Now the divided Confederate command system failed badly. Braxton Bragg, as liaison between Beauregard in the south and Lee in the north, should have kept Lee closely advised of Beauregard's problems but failed to do so. Beauregard didn't help matters because he didn't understand what was actually happening on his front and/or didn't report the facts to Lee. It was not until the 14th that Lee wrote to Davis: 'I think the enemy must be preparing to move south of James River. Our scouts and pickets yesterday stated that Genl Grant's whole army was in motion for the fords of the Chickahominy from Long Bridge down, from which I inferred that he was making his way to the James River as his new base. I cannot however learn positively that more than a small part of his army has crossed the Chickahominy.'

In fact the last of Grant's army crossed the James on 16 June, the same day Lee telegraphed Beauregard, 'Has Grant been seen crossing James River?' The troops defending Petersburg were able to hold off badly led and ill co-ordinated

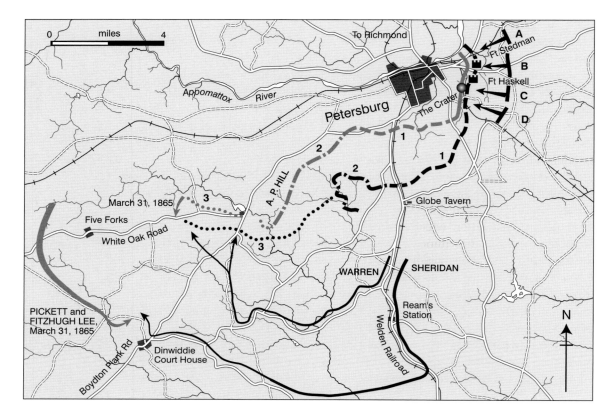

PETERSBURG

Initial Union assaults of 18 June 1864

A Neil and Martindale
B Birney
C Burnside
D Warren

1 Frontlines 21 August 1864

2 Frontlines Oct/Nov 1864 after Boydton Plank Road Operations

3 Frontlines 31 March 1865

Federal attacks on 16–17 June, but Beauregard realised that his opponent was numerically superior and finally called for help from Lee.

On the 17th, even while he was asking Beauregard, 'Can you ascertain anything of Grant's movements,' Lee ordered Hill's Corps into the lines at Petersburg. Lee himself arrived in the town that day. Now both armies started to dig in for a prolonged siege. Lee would no longer be able to use his one advantage, his ability to manoeuvre his troops in the field, and numbers would from now on count more than tactical or strategic abilities. Moreover, as he wrote to Davis on the 19th, 'My greatest apprehension at present is the maintenance of our communications south. It will be difficult, and I fear impracticable to preserve it uninterrupted.' Lee realised that, as he told Early before sending him towards Washington, once that happened, 'it will be a mere question of time'.

Grant just didn't dig in and wait for Lee to surrender or abandon his works. He continually sent off raids on railway lines all around Richmond. On the 21st he sent a major raid of both cavalry and infantry on the Southside Railroad and the Richmond & Danville that ran west of the city. Confederate troops caught up with them and took some 1,000 prisoners and thirteen cannon. On the 28th Grant sent an expedition north of the James and Lee was forced to rush troops to the fortifications there to block the raid. All the time both sides were sinking mines and counter-mines, but the biggest of them all was to be blown up on 30 July directly under a salient manned by South Carolina troops.

The mine, heard but not found by counter-mining Confederate engineers, created tremendous damage when it was detonated early that morning and Federal troops rushed into the gap in Lee's line. Luckily for him, the African-American troops chosen and trained for this attack had been replaced for political reasons at the last minute and the replacement white troops had no idea what to do when they reached the crater left by the explosion. As they milled around there, Confederate Major General William Mahone rushed troops into the gap, closing it, and killing Federal troops by the hundreds in the crater.

Federals attacked again north of the James on 14–16 August, and again were held by troops that Lee rushed there. On the 19th the Federals again attacked on the Weldon Railway, at Globe Tavern, just south of the Confederate right flank. Although the Confederates held there, the Federals destroyed a part of the railway and put it out of operation. On the 24th they attacked the railway again, destroying more tracks at Ream's Station before being driven back. Lee was not surprised, writing to Davis on 22 August, 'As I informed Your Excellency when we first reached Petersburg, I was doubtful of our ability to hold the Weldon road so as to use it.'

Although Grant was losing men steadily, he was still able to detach his VI Corps to hurry to Washington to block Early's raid towards that city from the Valley of Virginia. Early was forced to withdraw, and a Federal force including that corps, now led by Major General Philip Sheridan, pursued. Lee had also sent reinforcements to Early on 6 August, but Early's force was driven southward from point to point until by the end of October the Federals ruled the Valley, Early's command was no more, and he disappeared from the active Confederate army.

On 29 September Federal forces under Grant attacked and captured Fort Harrison, an important feature of the defensive line east of Richmond. Next day Lee personally directed an attack to retake Fort Harrison, but it failed. Longstreet, still partially paralysed, returned from recuperation in early October, meeting Lee whom he found 'worn by past labour, besides suffering at seasons from severe sciatica ...' Moreover, Longstreet wrote: 'After the loss of Fort Harrison, General Lee became more anxious for his line on the north side, and rode out to witness the operations on that front, under the threatening of Butler's forces ... His idea was that the north side was the easier route of Grant's triumphal march into Richmond, and that sooner or later he would make his effort in great force.'

Grant's main thrust, beginning in October, however, was west rather than north, on Lee's right flank. Such moves would force Lee to thin further his already slender lines. On 27 October he sent two corps across Hatcher's Run towards the Plank Road. The Confederates there under A. P. Hill held, but the Federals attacked at the same time east of Richmond along the Charles City and New Market Lines. Confederates held here, too.

But battle losses and desertions were sapping the strength of Lee's army. On 23 August he had begged the Secretary of War for more recruits, writing: 'Our numbers are daily decreasing … If we had here a few thousand men more to hold the stronger parts of our lines where an attack is least likely to be made, it would enable us to employ with good effect our veteran troops. Without some increase of our strength, I cannot see how we are to escape the natural military consequences of the enemy's numerical superiority.' In the meantime, on 5 December, the VI Corps rejoined the Army of the Potomac, fresh from its victories in the Valley. Lee recalled what numbers he could from Early's remaining command as well.

As 1865 opened Davis reassessed the situation, both military and political. He found himself under increasing pressure, as War Department Clerk J. B. Jones noted in his diary on 17 December that 'his enemies are assailing him bitterly, attributing all our misfortunes to his incompetence, etc. etc.' In the west Davis replaced Johnston by John B. Hood, a move that was condemned by both civilians and Hood's soldiers alike. Feelings against Davis were on the rise and on 27 December Jones noted in his diary, 'It is said Gen. Lee is to be invested with dictatorial powers, so far as our armies are concerned. This will inspire new confidence.' He added three days later, 'There is supposed to be a conspiracy on foot to transfer some of the powers of the Executive to Gen. Lee.'

Davis decided to nip these rumours in the bud by creating the post of Commanding General of the Armies of the Confederate States, a post held earlier by Winfield Scott in the U.S. Army. Congress, filled with politicians who despaired of Davis's ability to win the war, quickly authorised such a post with the understanding that Lee would be named to it. On 4 February 1865, Lee was notified that he had been confirmed in this post, and he accepted it, adding, however, that he had 'received no instructions as to my duties'. Lee officially assumed office on 9 February.

Interior of Fort Sedgewick ('Fort Hell'), Petersburg. Capt. Andrew J. Russell. (US National Archives)

Having been so involved in running his own theatre, he did not feel comfortable about issuing orders to other theatre commanders, writing to Davis that same day: 'I must, however, rely upon the several commanders for the conduct of the military operations with which they are charged, and hold them responsible.' Almost immediately Davis's political opponents, including Vice President Alexander H. Stevens, attempted to side-step Davis and have Lee make army commander appointments. Lee declined, writing to Stevens on February: 'I do not consider that my appointment as genl in Chief of the Armies of the Confederate States confers the right which you assume belongs to it, nor is it proper that it should. I can only employ such troops & officers as may be placed at my disposal by the War Department.' Lee would *not* become the military dictator of the Confederacy.

Moreover, it was evident to all in high command that soon there would be no Confederacy. In February Longstreet even went so far as to meet his counterpart on the other side of no man's land, Major General Edward Ord, commander of the Union Army of the James, to discuss the chance of Lee meeting Grant to seek a way to end the war. On 2 March Lee wrote to Grant: 'Sincerely desiring to leave nothing untried which may put an end to the calamities of war, I propose to meet you at such convenient time and place as you may designate, with the hope that upon an interchange of views it may be found practicable to submit the subjects of controversy between the belligerents to a convention of the kind mentioned.' Grant, however, replied that he had 'no authority to accede to your proposition for a conference on the subject proposed. Such authority is vested in the President of the United States alone.' At that point Lee realised that he would eventually have to surrender his beloved Army of Northern Virginia.

Yet, he felt duty bound to continue fighting until no chances were left. He would not surrender an intact fighting force in the field, including as it did the Army of Northern Virginia, numbering according to its returns of 1 March, 56,000 men, until absolutely necessary.

To the south, Sherman reached the Atlantic coast at Savannah in December, and after refitting, started pressing north through the Carolinas. Joseph Johnston was given the command of odds and sods, largely from local garrisons and the remainders of the Army of Tennessee. But this force could do no more than slow Sherman's steady advance. Lee had to do something.

As usual, Lee chose to attack. He found a point in the Union lines that was close enough to Confederate lines that an assault-party could reach quickly. Moreover, several posts behind the main objective, Fort Stedman, could be rapidly taken thereafter, splitting Grant's line in half and perhaps forcing him to give up the siege so that Lee could begin to manoeuvre once again. In the early morning hours of 25 March he launched an attack under the highly competent John B. Gordon. Supporting troops were slow to arrive, however, and Confederate intelligence was incorrect about the supposed posts behind Fort Stedman. The Federal reaction was quick and Union troops sent in to hold that

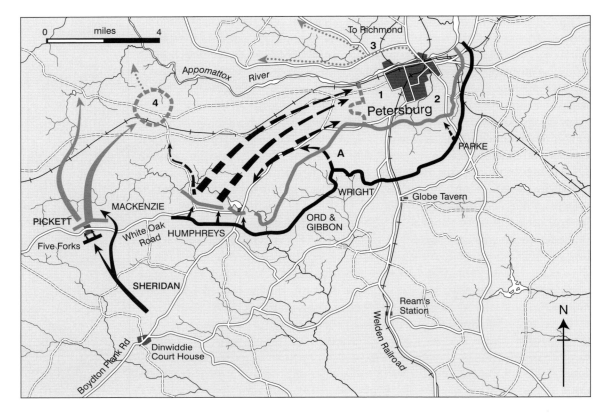

FIVE FORKS

A 2 April: decisive
    break-in by Wright

1 Longstreet
2 Gordon
3 Longstreet and
   Gordon withdraw
   night of 2/3 April
4 Anderson covering
   reorganisation of
   Pickett's command

line cut off the way between Fort Stedman and the main Confederate line with fire. Reinforcements could not cross to Gordon's men, and the latter found it too dangerous to attempt to get back to their lines. Losses, especially in the captured, were high. This would be Lee's last offensive move.

On 29 March Grant returned to worry Lee's right and Lee was forced to thin his lines yet more to meet this challenge, placing some 10,500 infantry and cavalry at Five Forks under George Pickett. Pickett's drive of 31 March started out well enough, pushing Federals under Philip Sheridan back towards Dinwiddie Court House before retiring back to Five Forks. There, on 1 April, while Pickett was enjoying some freshly caught shad with some of his generals, the Federals struck. The attack was so overwhelming that even if the generals had been at their posts the outcome would probably have been the same. However, the collapse of Lee's right meant that his only way of escape, to the west, could soon be cut. On 2 April another Federal attack on Hatcher's Run to the west again broke Lee's lines. A. P. Hill, riding on reconnaissance with one sergeant as an orderly, ran into several Federal infantrymen that morning and was mortally wounded. Lee's only option was to evacuate his lines and give up Richmond.

He telegraphed Davis on 2 April: 'I think it is absolutely necessary that we should abandon our position. I have given all the necessary orders on the subject to the troops, and the operation, though difficult, I hope will be performed successfully.' During the night of 2/3 Lee's men fell back and began to head westwards. His overall plan was to join with Johnston's troops and the merged force would be strong enough to turn on either Grant or Sherman.

The retreat was sloppy. Large numbers of men left the ranks when they drew near their home districts, especially those from Virginia and North Carolina. The army straggled, especially Ewell's Reserve Corps, which was drawn from the long-time defenders of Richmond who were unused to field service. Moreover Ewell's staff failed to get a pontoon bridge in place near the ruins of the Genito Road bridge in time for the head of his column to use. Lee was forced to wait at Amelia Court House on 4 April for his army to concentrate there. 'We stopped at Amelia all the morning reorganising commands, & waiting for the rear to close up,' recalled E. P. Alexander.

Instead of blaming Ewell and his staff, however, Lee offered the feeble, and obviously mendacious, excuse that because of not 'finding the supplies ordered to be placed there, nearly twenty-four hours were lost in endeavouring to collect … subsistence for men and horses. This delay was fatal, and could not be retrieved.'

The army headed west again towards Danville. On the morning of 6 April intelligence placed Union cavalry under Sheridan across their path. 'I never saw Gen. Lee seem so anxious to bring on a battle in my life as he seemed this afternoon,' recalled Alexander. Reconnaissance indicated that Sheridan's men, however, had been reinforced by infantry, making such an attack more likely to fail than succeed. 'That blocked our direct road to Danville,' wrote Alexander. 'But Gen. Lee hoped that by a rapid all night march he might pass Grant's flank & yet get ahead of him.'

Lee was everywhere during this desperate march. J. B. Gordon recalled that: 'General Lee was riding everywhere and watching everything, encouraging his brave men by his calm and cheerful bearing. He was often exposed to great danger from shells and bullets; but, in answer to protests, his reply was that he was obliged to see for himself what was going on.'

Lee watched as his troops filed by. 'Gen. Lee was with us very early,' Alexander wrote, '& I remember his getting very impatient & worried because the troops he was expecting to come up & pass us did not appear.' Nor would they do so. Grant's troops attacked Ewell's slow-moving garrison troops, who included sailors from the James River Flotilla, at Saylor's Creek. Attacked from three sides, Ewell's force disappeared in the action that followed, and lost Lee a large part of his remaining army.

On 7 April Lee's survivors reached Farmville. That evening he received a note from Grant, 'asking of you the surrender of that portion of the Confederate army known as the Army of Northern Virginia'. He sent back a message to Grant asking for terms. Lee's old artillery chief, William Pendleton, also reported that a number of top officers now believed that it was time to

Lee's other new corps commander after Jackson's death was Richard Ewell, later much criticised for his failure to take Cemetery Ridge at Gettysburg in the evening of 1 July.

surrender. Lee, however, was reported as replying, 'I trust that it has not come to that.'

Grant's reply of the 8th was that his only demand on surrender would be: 'that men and officers surrendered shall be disqualified from taking up arms against the government of the United States until properly exchanged'. Lee played for time, replying that he did not 'think the emergency has arisen to call for the surrender of this army', but agreed to meet 'on the old stage road to Richmond', at ten the next morning. At the same time, Lee learned that Grant's men were rapidly moving to surround the Army of Northern Virginia. Lee made one last try to see if his men could break through the Union circle. He sent cavalry under Fitzhugh Lee and infantry under J. B. Gordon to the attack. Initially successful, two Federal guns and a line of entrenchments fell to the Confederates. Federals quickly plugged the gap with both infantry and cavalry, and Gordon was forced to report to Lee's staff officer asking about the attack, 'I cannot long go forward.' On learning of this Lee said, 'There is nothing left for me but to go and see General Grant, and I had rather die a thousand deaths.' The attack was halted and white flags of truce began to appear over front-line units.

On the morning of the 9th, Alexander approached Lee, who told him that the Confederates were unable to cut their way out of the trap, and suggested that the army be ordered to scatter into the countryside and that each man should individually make his way to Johnston's army. Lee rejected this idea, pointing out that these men: 'would have to plunder & rob to procure subsistence. The country would be full of lawless bands in every part & a state of society would ensue from which it would take the country years to recover ... But it is still early in the spring, & if the men can be quietly & quickly returned to their homes there is time to plant crops & begin to repair the ravages of the war. That is what I must now try to bring about.' A crestfallen Alexander wrote that, 'I thought I had never half known before what a big heart & brain our general had.'

On 9 April Lee wrote to Grant asking for 'an interview, at such time and place as you may designate, to discuss the terms of surrender of this army ...' Shortly after noon he received Grant's note designating the front parlour of a house owned by Wilber McLean near Appomattox Court House. During his meeting with Grant there he pointed out that Confederate officers and men owned their horses, which would be needed for farming, and asked that they be allowed to keep them. Grant accepted this, and indeed went out of his way to avoid humiliating Lee and his officers and men, and the two quickly signed the surrender document. On 10 April Lee issued General Order No. 9, officially announcing the army's surrender, and received his own parole. On the 15th he returned to Richmond, a private citizen. His last official act was to write to Davis, then on the run south, that he did not believe that the Confederate government could be supported either by an army in Virginia or anywhere east of the Mississippi River. 'A partisan war may be continued, and hostilities protracted, causing individual suffering and the devastation of the country, but I see no prospect by that means of achieving a separate independence,' he wrote. 'To save useless effusion of blood, I would recommend measures be taken for suspension of hostilities and the restoration of peace.'

Appomattox Court House, Virginia, scene of Lee's surrender to Grant. Timothy O'Sullivan. (US War Dept.)

LEE'S GREATEST VICTORY: CHANCELLORSVILLE

A concerned Robert E. Lee looked to the possibilities for the spring 1863 campaign. Major William Norris, chief of Confederate intelligence, reported that the Army of the Potomac facing Lee's Army of Northern Virginia had between 150,000 and 160,000 men and, as he wrote to Longstreet on 27 April, it looked 'as if he intended to make an aggressive movement'. As Lee expected, his intelligence reports overstated enemy strengths. Even so, the Army of the Potomac reported 138,378 officers and men present for duty as of 30 April 1863. Returns of 31 March showed that Lee's army had 64,799 officers and men present for duty, so the Union forces had a significant advantage. In fact it would be the Army of the Potomac's largest numerical advantage in the war so far.

Moreover, because of the difficulties in supplying men and animals with food over the winter months, Lee had been forced to disperse his cavalry and send James Longstreet, his 'old war horse', with two divisions to Southside Virginia and down into North Carolina where they could forage as well as block potential Union threats. On 27 April Lee wrote to Longstreet explaining the Union threat and pointedly asking, 'Can you give me any idea when your operations will be completed and whether any of the troops you have in Carolina can be spared from there?' Longstreet, always keen on having an independent command, declined to take the hint. He instead asked for more troops to campaign across the Blackwater River towards Suffolk. Lee declined this request, but he would not have Longstreet's badly needed troops available to meet the first Union thrust of the spring, because Longstreet settled down to an eventually unsuccessful siege of Suffolk.

Although Lee was Longstreet's superior, he could not bring himself to order his subordinate to abandon his expedition and return his divisions to the main army, even though he knew he was facing a potentially overwhelming enemy force. Indeed, on 29 April he telegraphed Davis warning that: 'The enemy crossed the Rappahannock today in large numbers … I have learned this evening by couriers from Germanna & Ely's Fords that the enemy's cavalry crossed the Rapidan at those points about two (2) p.m. today. I could not learn their strength, but infantry was said to have crossed with the cavalry at the former point. Their attention I presume is to turn our left & probably to get into our rear. Our scattered condition favours their operations.' He added in a second telegraph, 'Longstreet's division, if available, had better come to me …' In fact, it would not.

Lee's advantage was his clear vision of what the enemy would do. As early as 12 March he had received information from local residents that the Union plan was to feint at his main line below Falmouth, while crossing further up the river, at the United States Ford and Falmouth. He therefore ordered the commander at the United States Ford to strengthen his works and try to learn all he could, possibly from enemy cavalry pickets who liked to exchange papers or tobacco with his pickets.

Lee saw the enemy's intentions well. The Army of the Potomac again had a new commander. After Ambrose Burnside's failures at Fredericksburg and the following attempt to flank Lee, Lincoln had replaced him by Joseph Hooker. Hooker, a corps commander in the Army of the Potomac, was disliked by his peers as a political plotter who aimed at taking Burnside's place as army commander. Lincoln even acknowledged Hooker's ambitions, but wrote to Hooker that he was willing to gamble on that if Hooker could bring about a victory.

Hooker's plan, which Lee anticipated, was simple, indeed not unlike Burnside's previously failed one. He would leave a force to threaten the Confederate lines at Fredericksburg, while taking the bulk of the Army of the Potomac around Lee's left flank. Once clear of the Wilderness area around Chancellorsville, he would force Lee either to abandon his line at Fredericksburg or attack Hooker's troops in a position of Hooker's choosing. Fredericksburg had shown what advantage lay in the hands of defending forces who were dug in. At the same time, Hooker sent off his cavalry, some 12,000 strong, on a long raid around Lee's army, towards Richmond, to destroy bridges, disrupt lines of supply and communications, and generally create mass confusion and fright. Lee, lacking cavalry, could spare only two regiments which would essentially observe the course of the raid and so hassle the Federal cavalry that they would not be too free to pillage at leisure.

On 27 April Hooker dispatched about half of his entire infantry force, three corps strong, westwards. They crossed the fords without much opposition, and by the evening of the 30th had some 75,000 men moving through the Wilderness, past Chancellorsville, into open ground some ten miles behind Lee's line. At the same time, Hooker left corps commander Major General Joseph Sedgwick with three corps, some 40,000 men, facing the Confederate works at Fredericksburg. Lee had to either retreat or offer battle at a tremendous disadvantage.

Always aggressive, Lee chose to fight. The result, later wrote E. P. Alexander, was a battle showing that: 'luck favoured pluck & skill, & how we extricated ourselves by the boldest & most daring strategy of the whole war; combined with some of the most beautiful fighting which it witnessed …' Although he had learned of Hooker's move, Lee had placed defensive forces under Richard Anderson to cover his left. Lee himself remained in Fredericksburg that evening, observing the Union forces crossing the river at Fredericksburg while he tried to determine whether the flank attack was merely a diversion, while the main attack would come at Fredericksburg, or was in fact the main attack. Jackson, still with him, argued for an attack on the Federals who were deploying on the southern side of the river before they could get wholly in position. Clouds at first hid the moon, but they soon blew away, leaving a bright evening in which it would be impossible to advance without being seen. Lee, having noted the large

Richard Anderson was Lee's last corps commander. Popular but lacking ambition, he was also a bit lazy and slow. (US National Archives)

concentration of Federal cannon covering the field between the two armies, finally gave approval only if Jackson could be sure that the attack would be successful.

On the 29th Lee decided to make his main effort on the flanking march. He issued Special Order No 121 by which McLaws' division would leave one brigade to hold the line behind Fredericksburg, while the remainder of his division would reinforce Anderson. Jackson would leave behind Early's division, and take the rest of his corps westwards as well. In the early morning of 1 May, leaving only a thinly held line at Fredericksburg of some 10,000 men commanded by Richard Ewell, Lee launched most of his troops westwards to confront Hooker's men.

As E. P. Alexander, commanding an artillery battery west of Fredericksburg, remembered that morning: 'Up the road from Fredericksburg comes marching a dense & swarming column of our shabby grey ranks, and at the head of them rode both General Lee & Stonewall Jackson. Immediately we knew that all our care & preparation at that point was work thrown away. We were not going to wait for the enemy to come & attack us in those lines, we were going out on the warpath after him. And the conjunction of Lee & Jackson at the head of the column meant that it was to be supreme effort, a union of audacity & desperation.'

At about 8 o'clock, Jackson arrived to take direct command of the Confederates digging-in across the Turnpike and Plank Road. This was the first time that Confederates in an open field spent the time before action in digging entrenchments, though they were handicapped by the lack of tools. This would later become standard practice in both armies during any halt. Jackson, realised that the troops he had there would be too weak numerically to hold long, and he decided to disrupt Hooker's advance by attacking. He ordered the men to stop digging and advance in column, led by McLaws' Division, down the turnpike that led straight to Chancellorsville, some five miles away. A second column, led by Carnot Posey's brigade, would advance along the Plank Road, running left of the Turnpike, south and then towards Chancellorsville, crossing the Turnpike at nearly right angles. The Confederates had gone from a passive defence to the attack.

The Confederate advance ran into the lead Federal elements near Zion Church on the road between Fredericksburg and Chancellorsville and some two miles out of the Wilderness. Here there was open ground where superior Union firepower, from both infantry and artillery, gave them a tremendous advantage. Jackson called up Alexander's artillery: 'Within a mile of the forks of the road we met the enemy's pickets, & from there on, our skirmish line kept up a lively fire with the enemy who fell back slowly, making all the delay that they could … In about *two* miles of Chancellorsville, we got into an extensive open country & at the far side of it we saw a great display of Hooker's force, & I brought up more guns, & more infantry was deployed, which we moved steadily forward towards

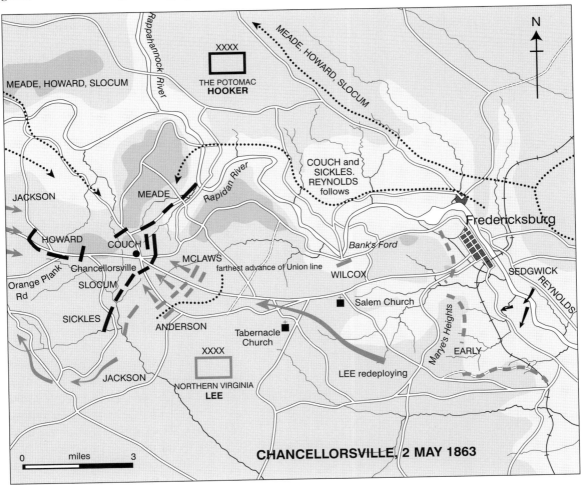

CHANCELLORSVILLE, 2 MAY 1863

them. But they soon began to disappear in the woods & we recognised that they were being withdrawn.'

Hooker's nerve failed. While his corps commanders called for him to fight there and then in the open, at about 2 p.m. he ordered them to fall back, into the heavily overgrown Wilderness area, to lines posted in a small clearing around Chancellorsville. The wooded area around it was so dense that an entire battalion could disappear from view after going a half dozen yards. However, an obviously shaken Hooker told Darius Couch, commander of the Union II Corps and next in line to take command of the Army of the Potomac should Hooker go, that he had 'Lee just where I want him; he must fight me on my own ground'. A sceptical Couch, however, later wrote that: 'to hear from his own lips that the advantages gained by the successful marches of his lieutenants were to culminate in fighting a defensive battle in that nest of thickets was too much, and I retired from his presence with the belief that my commanding general was a whipped man.'

Lee at Chancellorsville.

On the Plank Road, Posey's force ran into XII Corps skirmishers near the Alrich farmhouse. He drove them back until meeting a solid line of defence along the road leading to Catherine Furnace, below Chancellorsville. The Confederates then halted to form a full line of battle to face them. Jackson personally checked on this development, learning from A. P. Hill that Union resistance had significantly stiffened. Jackson sent a report of this back to Lee, and then returned to the fighting on the Turnpike. As darkness began to fall, Union forces dug entrenchments with their bayonets, tin cups, and plates to defend their lines around Chancellorsville.

Lee, however, was taken aback by this unexpected and unnecessary retreat. Was Hooker trying to draw him further and further away from Fredericksburg? He knew that he was still facing a much greater force than his own, and moreover was still caught in a potential vice. He cautiously sent out scouts and small reconnaissance parties to probe the Federal line. On the Confederate left, Stuart's cavalry had probed the Union right during the fight, and they were unopposed because Hooker had foolishly sent virtually all his cavalry on a long-range raid before the battle. Stuart reported that the Union line failed to connect with the Rapidan. Indeed, the position was carelessly defended and it would be possible to send a strong force down the road on which it sat and roll it up with ease.

Lee met Jackson that evening to discuss options for the next day. Jackson argued that Hooker realised his attack was no longer a surprise and was now retreating, adding, 'By tomorrow morning, there will not be any of them this side of the river.' Lee disagreed, pointing out that the scale of the attack indicated that it was too important to be that easily abandoned. They agreed that if Hooker were still there in the morning, the Confederates would have to press on their attack. The question was where. The direct road into the heart of Hooker's force seemed, from the day's fighting, to have been stiffened and would be costly and difficult, perhaps impossible, to take. The flanks seemed the only option, and Stuart's reports suggested a move on the Confederate left could be possible. The two sent their chief staff engineers to reconnoitre that ground.

Their reports suggested that Stuart was correct. But, armed with the up-to-date information provided by the various staff engineers and cavalry, Lee decided on a risky plan. When Jackson asked him where he should move the next morning, he simply stubbed a finger on the Federal right. Jackson knew exactly what to do and did not ask for, or receive, detailed tactical orders. The only thing Lee added was, 'General Stuart will cover your movement with his cavalry.' Jackson replied, 'My troops will move at 4 o'clock,' some four hours' time.

This is a perfect example of how Lee gave orders for a battle. He did not give specific instructions, merely a suggestion. He depended vitally on others to follow through. In the case of Jackson this worked beautifully; with others in later situations it would work less well.

Jackson left, and Lee spread out his saddle blanket, placing his saddle as a pillow. Before he could sleep, however, Jackson's chaplain, Tucker Lacy, whose brother lived nearby, came to tell Lee that the roads were indeed there to allow a flanking move. Then one of Jackson's aides woke him to tell him about his own reconnaissance on the Union right. 'Young men of my generation', Lee jokingly told him, 'would have done better in spotting the position of some annoying enemy artillery.' Lee then fell asleep and did not wake until sun-up.

Lee and Jackson met again to discuss the day's plan. Jackson then sent one of his scouts, civilian Jedediah Hotchkiss who served as a topographical engineer on Jackson's staff, to study the situation on the right. Hotchkiss noted in his diary: 'I went down to Mr. Welford's where General Stuart had his quarters, and ascertained the roads that led around to the enemy's rear and came back and reported to Generals Lee and Jackson ...' He returned to find Lee and Jackson sitting on boxes of captured Union army hardtack by a campfire at the junction of the Plank and Furnace Roads.

Hotchkiss' report was vital because Lee, although an engineer by training and prior experience, failed to ensure that his maps were detailed and accurate. Frankly the vague sketch maps he had of the area were unclear as to the roads around the Federal right. But Hotchkiss was able to show where a rough wagon trail ran just where wanted, ending at the Turnpike beyond the end of Hooker's line. Jackson told Lee that he would take his entire corps round by that way to strike Hooker's flank.

Lee's main defence would now be Early back at Fredericksburg, while he would have only McLaws' and Anderson's divisions of some 14,000 men to face Hooker's 65,000 troops who could drive directly at him while Jackson's 28,000 men were wandering around in the Wilderness. Lee considered Hooker's retreat of yesterday, finally deciding that the Union general was in much the same mental condition as McClellan had been when driven to the banks of the James River a year before. In short, there was no attack left in him, and Lee had not heard Sedgwick's footsteps coming from Fredericksburg. 'Well,' he told Jackson, 'go on!'

With that, Jackson started his troops. But much time had been lost and it was 7, not 4 a.m. when his lead elements passed Lee's headquarters, on their way down the road toward Catherine Furnace. As they marched by Jackson stopped for several minutes and chatted with Lee. Nobody recorded their conversation, and Jackson went on his way. Lee would never see his best general again.

Along the main line, Lee ordered artillery fire to provoke the enemy into counter-battery fire, which indicated that Hooker had not left overnight as Jackson had predicted. Indeed, he was remaining in the lines established the day

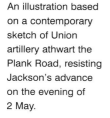

An illustration based on a contemporary sketch of Union artillery athwart the Plank Road, resisting Jackson's advance on the evening of 2 May.

before. In the meantime, Jackson's route took him south-westwards, then south for a couple of miles before turning right to reach the Brock Road. From there Jackson turned north through woods concealed from the enemy, before returning to the Brock Road.

Jackson's progress southwards did not go unobserved however. Reports of Confederates heading away from the battle reached Hooker's headquarters that morning. He hoped that this meant that Lee was doing what he wanted him to do, retreating. But he knew Lee's habits and retreating without a fight was not one of them. Noting the weakness of his right, he sent a message to the generals in command of his XI and XII Corps, O. O. Howard and Henry W. Slocum respectively: 'We have good reason to suppose that the enemy is moving to our right. Please advance your pickets for purposes of observation as far as may be safe in order to obtain information of their approach.' At the same time he sent an order to Sedgwick opposite Fredericksburg 'to attack the enemy to his front' if success seemed possible.

As Jackson's men passed by, Daniel Sickles, commander of III Corps, obtained permission to probe the Confederates to his front. His men struck the rear of Jackson's line of march at the Catherine Furnace. After some tough fighting that delayed Jackson's rear elements, the Confederates finally drove the Federals off and continued their line of march.

'It would seem that with only ten miles to go, & the roads being in average fair cross country-road condition, we should have reached our goal in five hours – say by 11 A.M.,' Alexander later wrote. 'But no one who has ever marched with a long column can form any conception how every little inequality of ground, & every mud hole, especially if the road be narrow, causes a column to string out & lose distance. So that, though the head may advance steadily, the rear has to alternately halt & start, & halt & start, in the most heartbreaking way, wearing out the men & consuming precious daylight, often beyond the calculations even of experienced soldiers … But here was a fighting column of only three divisions of Jackson's best men, with Jackson at their head, without baggage, but only ambulances & ordnance wagons, & with daylight worth a million dollars a minute, as will appear when we study the fight – starting at sunrise, which was about 5:10 A.M., and it took just 12 hours or till 5:10 P.M. to make their ten mile march, to form, & to begin the battle.'

As Jackson's men marched and the remaining men in front of Hooker skirmished, Lee's chief of staff, Colonel Robert H. Chilton, arrived at Early's headquarters to deliver an order to retreat towards Chancellorsville, leaving but a brigade in the works at Fredericksburg. Early argued that such a move would be clearly visible to the Federals across the lines, but Chilton insisted, and Early began moving his men out. As they reached the Plank Road intersection, however, he received a note from Lee that indicated that Chilton was in error. Indeed, Lee wrote that he did not expect Early to join the main force unless it was absolutely safe to do so. The mix-up was typical of the sloppy work performed all too often by Lee's amateur staff.

At this point Early decided to press on towards Lee, but soon information came that the Federals were advancing and would soon be able to capture the army's artillery reserve, left by Lee in the rear since the guns would not be useful in the Wilderness. 'I determined to return at once to my former position,' Early wrote, 'and accordingly halted the column, faced it about and moved back, sending my Adjutant General, Major Hale, to inform General Lee of the fact ... We regained our former lines without trouble about ten or eleven o'clock at night, throwing out skirmishers towards the River road.'

As Early's men were making their way back to Fredericksburg, Jackson's men neared their goal. Front-line Federal troops spotted the approaching Confederates and tried to alert their commanders. Racial prejudice damaged this effort, however. Most of the troops in XI Corps, which lay in Jackson's path, were Germans. Even though many of them had had military experience in European armies and wars, native-born Americans were disdainful of the 'Dutch'. Brigadier General Charles Devens, who commanded an XI Corps division, simply replied to such reports, 'You are frightened, sir,' and ignored them. When such reports finally went over Devens' head to Howard's headquarters they were again dismissed out of hand.

Sunset came at about 6.45 that evening, and it was soon quite dark in the dense Wilderness area. It was about 5 o'clock when Jackson's men reached their destination and began forming into two-man-deep battle lines from columns of four abreast. About fifteen minutes later Jackson was able to order a general advance.

With frightened deer, rabbits and turkeys fleeing ahead of them, the Confederates smashed into the Union troops who were busy cooking their supper. The panic among the unprepared troops was virtually total, although at some points individual Union units managed to form into battle lines and fight bravely, only to be forced to flee when Confederates turned both their flanks. Colonel Leopold von Gilsa made a typical report after the battle: 'I am obliged to express my thanks to the men of my brigade, with very few exceptions, for the bravery and coolness which they have shown in repulsing three attacks, and they retreated only after being attacked in front and from the rear at the same time; but I am also compelled to blame most of my line officers that they did not or could not rally their companies half a mile or a mile more back, no matter if it could be done under the protection of a second line ...'

Word of this attack soon reached Howard, who immediately rode to that part of his line to help rally the troops. But he was, unable to stop the rot and was forced to flee to the safety of his reserve artillery lines. On the Confederate side, as sounds of the attack reached Lee, he ordered a general push on the Federal positions all along the line. But the momentum was dying. Dusk was falling. Confederate infantrymen, most of whom had not received rations for 48 hours, were hungry and tired from their long march. Attacking units became mixed up in the woods and unit commanders lost control of their units. Front-line units finally were halted, while reinforcements were called up.

Yet the day's action had been remarkable successful. Jackson's lead elements had driven the Federals back past the Wilderness Church so the Army of the Potomac was essentially a thin line between Jackson's men and Lee's remaining troops. Jackson, however, wanted nothing less than the total destruction of that enemy army. Along the front lines, however, in the darkness, there was real confusion. Units from both sides, attempting to join up with others in their armies, stumbled into enemy lines. Nervous skirmishers fired at shadows all night.

It was into this confused scene that Jackson chose to take a small reconnaissance party. Wearing a black talma, or raincoat, at about 9.30, Jackson's party rode between two front-line North Carolina regiments. The infantrymen, seeing only the black shapes of horsemen crashing through the brush on their front, fired. While Jackson's chief topographical engineer was immediately killed, Jackson was hit three times. Help came immediately, and after first aid was given, the general, unable to walk any distance, was placed on a litter. Heading

A popular depiction of Jackson's death. In fact, he received his mortal wound from friendly fire while scouting in front of the rebel lines.

towards the rear, they came under fire from Federal artillery, attracted by the firing in their front. One of the litter-bearers was hit and Jackson was thrown to the ground. As he was again being helped from the field, Brigadier General Dorsey Pender saw him and told him he was planning to retire his line to be reformed. 'You must hold your ground, General Pender,' was Jackson's last field order. 'You must hold your ground, sir!'

A. P. Hill, the second senior commander, assumed command, but the same battery that had killed the litter-bearer took him out of action when a fragment struck him in the leg caused a temporary paralysis. Unable to ride, Hill sent for Stuart to assume command. Stuart arrived on the scene shortly and, learning of the confused situation, agreed that the attack should not be continued until dawn of 3 May. He ordered artillery to be brought up to support the attack. In the meantime news of Jackson's wounding reached a stricken Lee. Then, at about 3 a.m., he wrote to Stuart: 'It is necessary that the glorious victory thus far achieved be prosecuted with the utmost vigour, and the enemy given no time to rally. As soon, therefore, as it is possible, they must be pressed, so that we may unite the two wings of the army.

'Endeavour, therefore, to dispossess them of Chancellorsville, which will permit the union of the whole army.

'I shall myself proceed to join you as soon as I can make arrangements on this side, but let nothing delay the completion of the plan of driving the enemy from his rear and from his positions.'

About an hour later, Hotchkiss arrived bringing the news Lee had already heard, and then briefed the commander as to the situation on Jackson's, now Stuart's, front. In the meantime, Confederate commanders took advantage of the lull to reorganise, as did the Federals. They managed to pull into a circle around Chancellorsville itself, with III Corps somewhat in the advance holding the Hazel Grove. The III Corps was the main obstacle between the two wings of the Confederate army which were only some mile and a quarter apart. Hooker, looking over the position, thought it was too exposed and ordered Major General Dan Sickles, III Corps' commander, to retire into the main Federal lines.

Despite the fact that his men were able to catch only a couple of hours of sleep at best, Stuart ordered a general advance at 5.30, aiming for Lee's position. Sickles' men were in the way, but the Federals had already begun retiring, so only rear-guards met the Confederate advance. They were easily driven back, but then the Confederates ran into the rest of Sickles' entrenched men. Again and again the Confederate brigade advanced into these works, and again and again they were driven back. Both sides attacked and counter-attacked. Confederate losses were especially heavy; indeed, many units suffered most of their casualties in the fighting around Hazel Grove. The 2nd North Carolina lost 214 officers and men killed of the 340 who had gone into battle. The Federals reinforced their positions with units from other corps, while Stuart finally committed his reserves to the attack and brought up more artillery.

During this fighting, at about 9 a.m., a shell from one of those Confederate cannon struck a column of the Chancellor house, Hooker's headquarters. Hooker himself was hit by fragments of the column when it was struck, and fell senseless to the ground. Although he quickly recovered consciousness and tried to mount to resume command, he found himself unable to do so. Darius Couch assumed command of the Union army. Couch found Sickles' men hard pressed, the Union line finally crumbling against the steady Confederate pressure. He decided to bring up more artillery around the Chancellor house, where his final lines would be placed. He ordered Sickles, who wanted to try to retake his lost ground with the bayonet, to withdraw from his lines and fall back on the Chandler house.

With this, as well as Stuart's successful attacks, the two wings of the Confederate army finally united, and Lee rode over to the Hazel Grove plateau, arriving at about 10 o'clock. He could see that Stuart's attack was spent, exhausted and bloodied units no longer able to sustain such fighting. Even so, he ordered Stuart to continue to advance in conjunction with the troops on the Confederate right. Massed Confederate artillery blasted into the Chancellorsville area. Eighteen Federal guns around the Chancellor house returned fire with double loads of canister. They, and the rest of the Federal forces, were finally forced out of the Chancellor house area by 10.30. Lee then rode into the captured area, to be greeted by the cheers of his weary men. It would be Lee's finest moment. Through pure audacity, his greatly outnumbered troops had stopped and beaten back, at great cost, a much superior army. He took time to telegraph Jefferson Davis that the enemy was, 'dislodged from all his positions around Chancellorsville & driven back towards the Rappahannock, over which he is now retreating … We have again to thank almighty God for a great victory.'

In fact, the Federals were still in fighting order, with two corps available that had seen little action at all. Moreover, help for Hooker's force should have been

In 1864 Jubal Early, whom Lee called 'my bad old man', received Lee's orders to take a column up the Valley towards Washington in emulation of Jackson's 1862 Valley Campaign. Early got to the gates of Washington, but was then forced back. Finally his force was totally destroyed by Philip Sheridan's troops.

close at hand. That morning Hooker ordered Sedgwick at Fredericksburg to come up, adding, 'The enemy's right flank now rests near the plank road at Chancellorsville. You will attack at once.' While Lee's men were taking a well-deserved break, Sedgwick was on the move.

Bringing his army across the Rappahannock on pontoon bridges into Fredericksburg, below the Confederate lines, Sedgwick probed the defences and then decided on a direct attack. He had some 27,000 men, while Early's forces numbered some 12,000. At about 10.30 the Federals struck the line at Marye's Heights, so easily defended only the previous December. This time, however, the Confederate line was much thinner. Although they downed a large number of Federals, they were unable to hold, and Sedgwick quickly took the heights.

The Confederates fell back to a new line based on Leach's house, behind Lee's Hill. Sedgwick could have pursued and perhaps destroyed Early's forces, but instead followed his orders to attack Lee's rear at Chancellorsville. He therefore

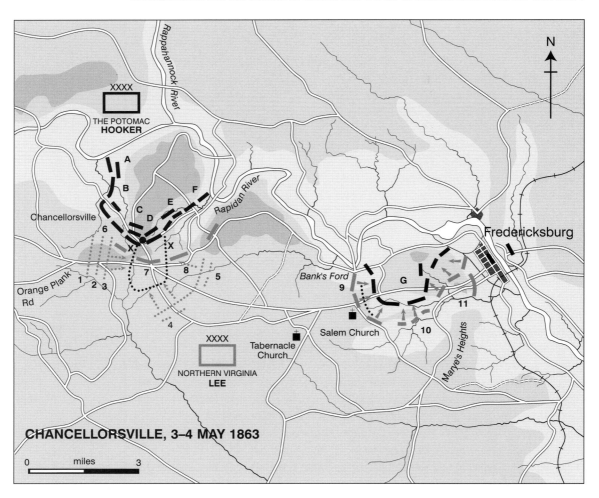

CHANCELLORSVILLE, 3–4 MAY 1863

0 miles 3

slipped around Early's left, heading westwards towards his goal. Early at the same time sent couriers to Lee with word of Sedgwick's success at Fredericksburg. News actually reached Lee before the Union's round-about telegraph system brought the news to Hooker.

Lee received word of this with the same calm that he had seen Scott display in a similar situation so many years earlier in Mexico, but he was aware of the potential danger that this move threatened. He decided to split his army again, believing that he had scared Hooker into inaction as earlier he had scared McClellan on the Peninsula. Leaving only a token force to keep the Federals busy along their new lines, he ordered McLaws' Division to turn and head eastwards to meet Sedgwick. At the same time, he ordered a Confederate division to advance up the U.S. Ford Road to keep the enemy off balance and prevent a Union attack. He sent another division north to the River Road to block the Mine Road junction and threaten the Union line of retreat across the river.

As Lee's troops came up, the Confederates in Sedgwick's front, under Cadmus M. Wilcox, an infantry tactics instructor at West Point before the war, fought a delaying action, falling back from point to point where the ground was most advantageous. Finally, they entrenched at Salem Church, a point on the Orange Plank Road five miles west of Fredericksburg and six miles east of Chancellorsville. Entrenchments there dated from a potential fall-back position dug during the Fredericksburg battle. At about 5 o'clock both forces were in position, and the Federals launched their attack. The back and forth fighting was heavy, but Lee had actually managed to concentrate more fighting men in the area than Sedgwick had been able to do.

The remainder of the troops who had garrisoned Fredericksburg, under Jubal Early, fell back southwards, where they were poised on Sedgwick's left. As fighting at Salem Church progressed, Lee ordered Early to 'come upon their left flank [linking up with Confederates already fighting and] … demolish them'.

But darkness had fallen now, and rather than risk a dangerous night attack Early advised McLaws that he would instead retake Marye's Heights to cut off Sedgwick's line of retreat there. Lee agreed, and made the point that it was important that McLaws hit Sedgwick the next morning so that Early could move unobstructed. That night on the Union side Hooker telegraphed Sedgwick, 'I believe the enemy has been reinforcing all night, and will attack me in the morning.' Obviously Sedgwick could expect no hope from Lee's rear, especially after Hooker telegraphed him, 'Look well to the safety of your corps …'

Next morning Early launched his attack on Marye's Heights. 'It was my purpose,' he later wrote, 'as soon as the heights were taken and the enemy's connection with Fredericksburg cut, to advance with Gordon and Smith's brigades up the Plank road and river, and for Hays and Hoke to advance across towards the plank road extending to the left to connect with McLaws, while Barksdale's brigade and some of Pendleton's artillery should be posted to hold Marye's and Lee's

Confederates Morning of 3rd:
1 Rodes
2 Colston
3 Heth
4 Anderson
5 McLaws

Afternoon of 3rd, 4th:
6 Heth
7 Rodes
8 Colston
9 McLaws
10 Anderson
11 Early

X … X Union frontline early 3 May
A Reynolds
B Meade
C Sickles
D Couch
E Howard
F Slocum
G Sedgwick

Hills and protect my rear from the direction of Fredericksburg.' Sedgwick's men would be trapped.

The Confederates quickly took the heights. Although a strong Federal force was stationed in Fredericksburg itself, the two sides neutralised each other and Sedgwick was now cut off. Early was listening for sounds of McLaws' advance but heard nothing. But he then left troops to contain the Federals at Fredericksburg, and headed towards Sedgwick's position. He also sent word to McLaws to advance, but McLaws, concerned with losses, chose to wait until Anderson's division arrived. Lee himself rode ahead of Anderson, reaching the front lines at about 11 o'clock. There he was dismayed to learn that McLaws, a cautious fighter at best, had failed to reconnoitre Sedgwick's lines or to deploy his troops for the attack. Moreover, Anderson's weary men were coming only slowly to their position. As they filed into position across ravine-cut country, Lee rode over to Early to confirm the attack.

At 6 o'clock everyone was in position and three cannon shots announced the attack. Fighting was fierce through thick woods that made co-ordination almost impossible. Sedgwick's men had to fall back and the lines around them were tightened, but his corps had not been destroyed. Lee decided on a rare night attack, but Sedgwick had had enough. With Hooker's approval, he ordered a general withdrawal northwards to Scott's Ford. The Confederates, delayed by his rear-guards, could advance only slowly in a night made darker by fog that settled over the area. The morning of 5 May brought news to Lee that Sedgwick's men had escaped, and Fredericksburg had been evacuated.

While Lee was trying to put together a night attack, Hooker met his corps commanders. Most of them wanted to stay and fight, but Hooker decided to retreat back across the river. Lee then sent most of his men in the area back to Chancellorsville, but a huge thunderstorm slowed their march on the muddy roads. Hooker took advantage of this weather to start his troops over the pontoon bridges laid across the rising river. At 7 p.m. the artillery began to cross, followed by the infantry. The V Corps served as a rear-guard, falling back to ever narrowing lines as the army crossed the river.

Lee was aware of this, but thought that Hooker was determined to make a last stand. He gave orders for an attack the following morning, but in the early hours of the 6th received word that the Federals were gone. A disgusted Lee exclaimed to Dorsey Pender, who brought him the news: 'Why, General Pender! That's the way you young men always do. You allow those people to get away. I tell you what to do, but you don't do it! Go after them! Damage them all you can!' But it was too late. The battle of Chancellorsville, incomplete in terms of what could have been the total destruction of the Union Army, was over and so was what had been Lee's greatest fight.

LEE AS A MILITARY STRATEGIST AND TACTICIAN

'My chief is first rate in his sphere – that of a commanding general,' Lee's adjutant Walter Taylor wrote home in March 1864. 'He has what few others possess, a head capable of planning a campaign and the ability to arrange for a battle, but he is not quick enough for such little affairs as the one I have described [a small raid in Madison County shortly before]. He must have good lieutenants, men to move quickly, men of nerve such as Jackson. With such to execute and the Genl to plan, we could accomplish anything within the scope of human powers.'

Indeed, Lee's tactical battlefield record is spotty, with brilliant victories such as Chancellorsville tempered with victories that could have been greater such as Second Manassas and outright defeats such as Gettysburg. On the whole Lee was not an especially good battlefield tactician, often because of his inability to give his subordinates direct orders and ensure that they were carried out.

For example, he had a great opportunity at the Second Manassas to destroy a large part of John Pope's army by attacking the Federal left. He could have rolled up Pope's line, forcing him to retreat across the single bridge crossing the Bull Run (which had been blocked in the 1861 battle by a wagon disabled by an artillery shot). But Longstreet, not having been pressed by Lee, did not attack, later claiming that a Federal corps under Fitz-John Porter was threatening him from the south. In fact, despite Pope's orders for Porter to bring his corps up, it hadn't moved and consequently presented no danger.

On 30 August 1862, Lee explained his lack of such an attack to Davis, 'my desire has been to avoid a general engagement, being the weaker force, & by manoeuvring to relieve the portion of the country referred to.'

Worse than that, in terms of tactical ability, was the battle he conducted at Gettysburg. There Longstreet, who disagreed with Lee's tactics in person at the battle and on paper afterwards, noted that he 'was excited and off his balance … and he laboured under that oppression …' Nobody else near Lee noted any especial excitement on the part of the general, but it is apparent that he grew too dependent on the sheer fighting ability of his men against the Army of the Potomac, especially after Chancellorsville.

In terms of strategy the picture is equally dark. It is obvious that he and Davis had different theories of strategy. Davis wanted to defend the Confederacy at every threatened point; he thought that the war could be won if the South simply didn't lose. Lee, on the other hand, thought that if the Confederacy were to win it would have to be quickly, before full Northern resources could be brought to bear. This would mean aggressive attacks designed to bleed Federal forces to the point where the Northern public would no longer support the war. At this point Lee was thinking that the South must not merely avoid defeat, but must actually win the war. Davis believed in concentrating forces at threatened points to halt each invasion, while Lee liked to divide his forces so as to draw the enemy apart and confuse him. Davis wanted to react to an enemy movement, attacking him at each point where he threatened Southern territory. Lee liked to have room for manoeuvre, and to drive an enemy back without actually fighting if possible. When working together, however, Davis so trusted Lee, that he allowed him to have his own way for the most part, while he was troubled by armies commanded by Joseph Johnston that acted in a way more conforming to Davis's strategic thinking. In modern business terms, Davis was strategically reactive, while Lee was proactive. In the end Davis favoured Lee's approach rather than Johnston's.

Many historians have blamed Lee for concentrating on his own theatre of operation and ignoring the western theatre except for his habit of getting rid of officers he distrusted to that theatre. This is, however, generally unfair since he was given the direct command of the eastern theatre and was not responsible until the very end, when it was too late, for overall direction of the war. By the time he was given such command, with Sherman's men bulldozing their way north through the Carolinas and the Army of the Potomac pinning him down in a hopeless siege at Petersburg, he knew it was too late to do much of real value.

When the new Secretary of War John Breckinridge asked for a strategic overview in March 1865, having just arrived at his post, General-in-Chief, half of Lee's reply was devoted to the difficulties he was having in supplying

his own army. On Johnston's army in the Carolinas, he wrote that 'its condition gives no strong prospect of a marked success'. Of the forces in the deep South east of the Mississippi River, he wrote merely that they were 'numerically inferior to those of the enemy', and added that he did not think they could be made 'adequate to the performance of the services that they will probably be called upon to render during the approaching campaign'. He made no mention of the Trans-Mississippi Department. Nor did he suggest any overall strategy to solve the problems he had noted, hopelessly ending that he believed that only the will of the people could bring success.

The only time one can therefore accurately judge his strategic abilities is during the period March to May 1862, when he was serving as military adviser to Jefferson Davis. Here, of course, he was not able to command directly, but merely make suggestions to field commanders as well as Davis himself. However, after the war Davis described Lee as being 'in general charge of army operations ...'

Lee faced an immediate problem when McClellan's Army of the Potomac, moving westwards along the Peninsula towards Richmond, was confronted by Joseph Johnston's Army of Virginia. His first job in the eastern theatre was to oversee operational level co-ordination between the troops already on the Peninsula when McClellan landed, and Johnston's troops, then facing towards Washington to counter any threat from that area. He also attempted to get the Confederate Navy to co-operate, writing to the Secretary of the Navy on 8 April 1862, to suggest moving the ironclad C.S.S. *Virginia* past Fort Monroe to the York River where she could destroy Union transports and defend that flank of the land-based troops.

Given his preoccupation with his commanders in the eastern theatre, Lee did not spend much time thinking about operations in the west, despite the fact that major events were taking place there. Fort Pulaski, gateway to Savannah, Georgia, fell on 11 April. A Confederate invasion of New Mexico and Arizona failed. New Orleans, one of the Confederacy's two major cities and production centres, fell. Fort Macon, North Carolina, was captured. Albert Sidney Johnson concentrated his forces there in April, striking U. S. Grant's army at Shiloh in what became a major southern defeat, Johnson losing his life in the battle. The Federals then slowly moved on Corinth, Mississippi.

Lee's sole contribution in terms of strategy or even operational oversight during this period, was one letter written on April and ordering General John C. Pemberton, then commanding general of the Department of South Carolina, Georgia, and Florida, to 'send, if possible, Donelson's brigade of two regiments to Corinth,' adding, 'If Mississippi Valley is lost Atlantic states will be ruined.' Obviously his main concern with a western Union offensive was how it would damage Virginia's chances of victory. Indeed, during his tenure of service as military adviser, this was the only letter he sent to any western commander.

Elsewhere he showed more concern with Virginia's defences, suggesting a number of moves to Major Generals Thomas J. Jackson, Edward Johnson, and

Henry Heth whose troops faced possible threats at different points in the Shenandoah Valley.

Finally, while his conversations with Jefferson Davis cannot be known, he left nothing in writing that would indicate that he ever formed an overall strategy to defend the Confederacy. Davis, in his post-war memoirs, never mentions discussing overall strategy with Lee. However, as he considered himself Commander-in-Chief in practice as much as in theory, he probably would not have done so. He does mention that Lee spent time supervising the building of works around Richmond for its defence during his time as military adviser – hardly the work of a master overall strategist.

Taylor suggests that the one sphere in terms of strategy and tactics where Lee excelled was at the operational level, where he planned moves for his particular army, created an atmosphere of mutual trust between himself, his subordinates, and the men in the ranks, and supervised the actual fighting on the battlefield.

Based on his original feeling that he had to out-manoeuvre his enemy, while inflicting heavy enough casualties to make the Northern public no longer support the war, he planned and led two raids on the North. As he explained to Davis on 5 September 1862, when launching his first raid: 'Whatever success may attend that effort [the recruitment of Marylanders into the Army of the Potomac], I hope at any rate to annoy and harass the enemy.' At this type of raid he was at his best, proposing the general plan and indicating in a vague manner what his subordinates were to do, and then standing back and letting them do it.

His ability to manoeuvre was also tested in both the late 1863 campaigns where Meade, with his Army of the Potomac, attempted to force him into a position where he could be defeated, and in the 1864 campaign from the Wilderness to Petersburg where, at least until Grant crossed below Richmond towards Petersburg and thereby stole a march, he was successful in countering every Union move. This was Lee at his very best.

Indeed, his faith in manoeuvre as a means of relieving threatened areas by unsettling Federal planners was so strong that even while he was facing McClellan's army on the Peninsula he wrote a telling letter to Davis on 5 June 1862: 'After much reflection I think if it was possible to reinforce Jackson [in the Shenandoah Valley] strongly, it would change the character of the war. This can only be done by the troops in Georgia, South Carolina & North Carolina. Jackson could in that event cross Maryland into Pennsylvania. It would call all the enemy from our Southern coast & liberate those states. If these states will give up their troops I think it can be done. McClellan will make this a battle of posts. He will take position from position, under cover of his heavy guns, & we cannot get at him without storming his works, which with our new troops is extremely hazardous … It will require 100,000 men to resist the regular siege of Richmond, which perhaps would only prolong not save it. I am preparing a line that I can hold with part of our forces in front, while with the rest I will endeavour to make a diversion to bring McClellan out.'

This was a classic example of Lee's concept of war-winning strategy on the Virginia front. It also gives a hint of the idea he had had all along that if he were pinned down in a siege, as would happen at Petersburg in 1864 with rather fewer than 100,000 men in his army, he would eventually lose.

He was also at his best at being at the right front-line spot and doing the right thing to encourage his troops. While defeated, wounded, and weary Confederates were returning to their lines after the assault of 3 July 1863, Lee was there. As Alexander saw: 'A great many of Pickett's fugitives passed by us, & Gen. Lee spoke to nearly all, telling them not to be discouraged, & saying, "Form your ranks now. We want all good men to hold together now." He also used the expression, "It was all my fault this time."' Likewise, he appeared time and again at threatened points during the fighting in the Wilderness in May 1864, encouraging and directing his front-line troops.

Barlows' Knoll, Gettysburg, north-west of the town. (US National Archives)

5

LEE, THE MANAGER

The commander of the Army of Northern Virginia had a number of management jobs to perform. First, he had to manage his boss, Jefferson Davis, so that he could get the job done as he wanted. This was no inconsiderable task. Davis insisted on fulfilling the position that the Confederate constitution spelled out, that of Commander-in-Chief. He was in many ways a micromanager, and insisted on close supervision of his subordinates, ignoring the Secretary of War to deal directly with field commanders. His was also a rigid personality, a man who had strong opinions and would rather argue with those who disagreed with him than try to work out a compromise. With some commanders this did not work at all. Joseph Johnston, although a favourite with the officers and men in the army, failed to manage Davis well and was, as a result, always on the outs with the president. Lee, on the other hand, managed Davis well.

Davis was extremely self-confident in his military abilities, and Lee, one could say, played up to this. 'I know that your visit [to the western theatre] has inspired the people with confidence, & encouraged them to renewed exertions & greater sacrifices in the defence of the country, & I attribute mainly the great victory of Genl Bragg [at Chickamauga] to the courage diffused by your cheering words & presence,' he wrote to Davis on 6 January 1863. A Joseph Johnston or a Pierre Beauregard would never have descended to such flattery.

Lee also went out of his way to keep the President informed. For example, in the month of January 1863, when little was happening on his immediate front, he wrote to Davis, not just the War Department, on the 6th, the 13th, 19th and 23rd. His letters were not simply short yes and no affairs, but long messages that spelled out in detail information on the enemy and his current and future plans. Showering Davis with letters that spelled out in detail everything concerning the army meant that Davis could not spend much time thinking about the overall situation and coming up with orders and plans with which Lee could disagree.

Next Lee had to manage his immediate subordinates: corps commanders Jackson, Longstreet, A. P. Hill, Ewell and Anderson, as well as his own staff. Here he adopted a 'hands off' approach, giving them a general idea of what he wished to happen and then leaving them to get it done as best they could. A British army observer at Gettysburg was amazed to watch him at Gettysburg while Confederate attacks were under way: 'During the whole time the firing continued he only sent one message, and only received one report. It is evidently his system to arrange the plan thoroughly with the three corps commanders, and then leave to them the duty of modifying and carrying it out to he best of their abilities.' Lee himself told visiting Prussian officer Justus Scheibert that he made plans and brought troops to the field; 'the rest must be done by my generals and their troops, trusting to Providence for the victory'.

Having allowed this freedom of action to his subordinates, Lee was careful not to chastise them too much if they made mistakes. When Stuart finally arrived at Gettysburg, his cavalry's absence having led to the fight, Lee met his wayward general and said only, 'Well, General, you are here at last.' Stuart understood this to be as severe a rebuke as Lee would ever make and was accordingly mortified. In much the same way, at Bristoe Station in October 1863, A. P. Hill, without adequate reconnaissance, launched a major attack into a strong Union position and was beaten back with large losses. Riding over the field the next day, Lee's rebuke was a simple, 'Well, General, bury your dead and let us say no more about it.' Lee later covered for Hill with the War Department, endorsing Hill's official post-action report: 'General Hill explains how, in his haste to attack the Third Army Corps of the enemy, he overlooked the presence of the Second, which was the cause of the disaster that ensued.'

In much the same way, he largely let his subordinates arrange their own commands as they felt best. For example, although it was no problem in his staff, others of his generals, such as Richard Ewell, placed relatives on their staffs, something Lee felt was a bad practice. He wrote home in February 1864 that 'I am opposed to officers surrounding themselves with their sons & relatives. It is wrong in principle & in that case the selection for offices would be made from private & social relations, rather than the public good.' Nevertheless he took no action against those relatives on his subordinates' staffs.

The men who usually were the intermediaries between Lee and his field subordinates were his staff officers. Brigadier General Moxley Sorrel, who had earlier served on Longstreet's staff, later called Lee's staff 'small and efficient'. Sorrel recalled: 'Four majors (afterwards lieutenant colonels and colonels) did his principal work … Of course it does not include the important administrative officers like Cole, chief commissary; Corley, chief quartermaster; Doctor Guild, medical director, and his chiefs of ordnance and other organisations.' Indeed, Sorrel noted that after the war: 'some hundreds of men in the South … call themselves members of Lee's staff, and so they were if teamsters, sentry men, detailed quartermasters (commissary men), couriers and orderlies, and all the rest of the following of a general headquarters of a great army are to be so considered. But by staff we usually confine ourselves to those responsible officers immediately about a general, and Lee had selected carefully.' In fact in the winter of 1863–64 Lee managed with a personal staff of only three men, although he did call on specialists for specific jobs.

With his immediate staff Lee often seemed inconsiderate, simply expecting them to get the things he wanted done without any extra supervision or praise. Moreover, the smallness of the staff guaranteed much overtime for them. Acting Assistant Adjutant-General Walter Taylor of his staff complained home on 8 August 1863, 'I never worked so hard to please any one, and with so little effect as with General Lee. He is so *unappreciative*.' In November 1863 he again complained, 'The truth is Genl. Lee doesn't make *our time pleasant here* & when promotion is offered his staff elsewhere, it is not to be wondered at if they accept the offer.' In August 1864, after describing an argument between the two, Taylor wrote that he couldn't help losing his temper because Lee 'is so unreasonable and provoking at times. I might serve under him for ten years to come and couldn't *love* him at the end of that period.'

Aware of his staff's lack of devotion from time to time, Lee explained it away in a letter to his wife dated 14 February 1864, 'The young men have no fondness for the society of the old Genl. He is too sombre & heavy for them.'

At the same time, he had good grounds for being frustrated by his staff and their work. They were mostly not professionals. Chief of Staff Robert Chilton, a West Point graduate, had been a staff officer in the U.S. Army before the war, but the only other professional soldier on the staff, *aide-de-camp* Armistead L. Long, another West Pointer, had had only line experience in the U.S. Army's artillery. *Aide-de-camp* Charles Venable was a college professor with no military experience before the war. Walter Taylor had been educated at the Virginia Military Institute but had spent no time in the active army, and became a businessman after his graduation. Charles Marshall had been a lawyer. Henry McClellan, who

A harvest of death – Gettysburg, July 1863. Timothy O'Sullivan. (US War Dept.)

switched to Lee's staff from Stuart's after the cavalry general's death, had been a schoolteacher. Giles Cooke, who joined the staff in 1864, had been a lawyer.

So Lee had to manage the entire Army of Northern Virginia with this small group, most of whom were amateurs. On 21 March 1863, he wrote to Davis that present staffs were not sufficient for the job. 'The greatest difficulty I find is in causing orders and regulations to be obeyed. This arises not from a spirit of disobedience, but from ignorance. We therefore have need of a corps of officers to teach others their duty, see to the observance of orders, and to the regularity and precision of all movements. This is accomplished in the French service by their staff corps, educated, instructed, and practised for the purpose. The same circumstances that produced that corps exist in our own Army. Can you not shape the staff of our Army to produce equally good results?'

In fact, Davis had neither time nor opportunity to pursue Lee's request, and Lee was forced to continue with his small group of on-the-job learners. But he felt that orders transmitted through the staff did not require his personal supervision; but required him to be essentially the inspiration of the army so that he could get it to perform to his will as directed by subordinates through the chain of command.

Unlike his mentor Winfield Scott, Lee did not consider that pomp, fancy full dress and large *entourages* would impress and inspire his men. Indeed, his personal dress style in the field was modest. Sergeant Major C. C. Cummings, 17th Mississippi Infantry, saw Lee in early June 1863: 'He wore a long linen duster, which so enveloped his uniform as to make it invisible … and he wore a wide-brimmed straw hat, evidently the art of his many lady admirers, all of which gave him the appearance of an old plain farmer.'

Nor did he delight in reviews and parades for their own sake, knowing how little the men appreciated them. When Longstreet's Corps returned from Tennessee in 1864, E. P. Alexander recalled: 'Lee honoured our return to his command with a review. It was the first review held since the Shenandoah Valley after Sharpsburg in '62. Gen. Lee was not given to parades merely for show. Now, I am sure, he felt & reciprocated the stirrings of that deep affection in the hearts of his men inseparable from our return upon the eve of what all felt must be the struggle to the finish. It was the last review he ever held …' In fact, out of concern for his soldiers, when Stuart in an attempt to impress his chief held a dress parade after Chancellorsville, complete with sabre charges and the firing of cannon, Lee forbade his cavalry from going faster than a march and his cannoneers from firing, to save their strength.

Stories about his care for his men quickly spread through the ranks. General John B. Gordon told one such story in which Lee saw a weary soldier near his tent and called out to him:

'"Come in captain, and take a seat."

'"I'm no captain, general; I'm nothing but a private," replied the embarrassed soldier.

'"Come in, sir," Lee replied. "Come in and take a seat. You ought to be a captain."'

Lee's concern for this common soldier was noticed by the men. Private John Worsham, 21st Virginia, was in the ranks for the 1861 West Virginia Campaign and recalled that Lee's headquarters was only a couple of hundred yards from Worsham's unit. There Lee 'soon won the affection of all by this politeness and notice of the soldiers. He very often had something to say to the men; and it soon became known that when some of the people in the neighbourhood sent him something good to eat, the articles were sent to some sick soldier as soon as the messenger got out of sight. This affection increased as the years rolled on, and I suppose no body of men under his command had more love and respect for our great leader than those men who first served under him.'

At Spotsylvania Court House, Worsham saw Lee standing by the side of the road as his unit marched by. 'As our column approached him, an old private stepped out of ranks and advanced to General Lee. They shook hands like acquaintances and entered into a lively conversation. As I moved on, I looked back, and the old man, still talking, had his gun in one hand and the other on Traveller's [Lee's horse] neck. It was scenes such as this that made General Lee so popular.'

This concern was honest, not put on for the benefit of his public. On 26 September 1861, in the pouring rain of West Virginia, Lee wrote to his wife that his men were without tents, adding, 'I fear I shall not sleep for thinking of the poor men.' His wife often knitted socks, despite her rheumatism, and he delighted in passing on her products to the rank-and-file.

No detail was too small to catch his eye. On 10 June 1862, shortly after taking command of the Army of Northern Virginia, he wrote to the army's quarter-master-general, 'This army has with it in the field little or no protection from the weather. Tents seem to have been abandoned, and the men cover themselves by means of their blankets & other contrivances. The shelter tent … manufactured out of the tents now on hand [would be] better than what they have in use. A simple fly or cloth of that shape would answer the purpose. This continued inclement weather I fear will produce great sickness & I desire to see what can be done for the protection and comfort of the men.'

Of course his record in repeatedly repelling the enemy, and his victories in the field, also encouraged his men. In the end, Lee was able to manage an army that trusted him completely to take care of it.

The result was summed-up by Alexander: 'I am sure there can never have been an army with more supreme confidence in its commander than that army had in Gen. Lee. We looked forward to victory under him as confidently as to successive sunrises.'

6

LEE AND THE WEAPONS OF WAR

Lee was educated and had seen active service as a staff engineer. He spent a brief time as a field grade officer in a cavalry regiment. Yet he was at heart an infantry-man. He relied chiefly on his infantry, armed with single-shot, muzzle-loading rifled muskets, to fight his battles, employing artillery, cavalry, and engineers only in their support. If he had a chance to take advantage of new weapons, organisations, or systems technology that required different services, he tended to reject this technology in favour of his tried and true infantry.

European armies at the time included a number of varieties of infantry units, each with distinctive uniforms, weapons, and purposes. The French had *voltigeurs*, line infantry, *chasseurs*, and *Zouaves*; the British Army had line infantry and special rifle regiments. Lee preferred all his units to be regular, line infantry. In April 1862, seeing the success of a handful of Union units called sharpshooters, who were clad and used much as British rifle regiments, the Confederate Congress authorised each infantry brigade to pull men from line units to form a special sharpshooter battalion. This would be armed with long-range weapons and used for skirmishing and as shock troops. Although it was late for these units to be organised, armed, and trained for the 1862 campaign-ing season, Confederate commanders in their other great army, the Army of Tennessee, used that winter to organise them and fielded a number of these units in the 1863 campaign.

In Lee's army, however, the idea was largely ignored for the 1863 campaign. One such unit was formed in the Shenandoah Valley, away from Lee's direct control, in August 1862. Other attempts in the Army of Virginia, such as the Palmetto Sharpshooters, were quickly turned into Lee's favoured regular line infantry. It was not until Longstreet's Corps was sent west in late 1863 that sharp-shooter battalions were added to the Army of Northern Virginia's rosters, and that only in Longstreet's Corps, which saw service in the west when the battalions were added. Finally, during the winter of 1863–64, a number of Lee's brigade commanders, seeing the possibilities, began to organising their own units of various strengths. Lee neither encouraged nor discouraged this new develop-ment, and the units were used as ordered at divisional and brigade level, rather than at an army level.

Baron de Jomini, in his standard text of the time, *The Art of War*, wrote of cav-alry that it could: 'never defend a position without the support of infantry. Its chief duty is to open the way for gaining a victory, or to render it complete by carrying off prisoners and trophies, pursuing the enemy, rapidly succouring a threatened point, overthrowing disordered infantry, covering retreats of infantry and artillery.' Indeed such a sabre charge on wavering infantry at the First Manassas, a battle Lee missed, gained fame for Stuart and his Virginia cavalry regiment.

The Enfield Pattern 0.577-calibre Infantry Rifle Musket was a typical weapon arming the infantry of both sides .

Lee ignored Jomini's advice. Under standard European practice, for example, Lee would have had cavalry ready, following up his assault at Gettysburg on 3 July 1863, to follow up the breakthrough on the Federal lines. Instead he sent Stuart's cavalry round the flank to attack Federal cavalry there. Visiting British officer Arthur Fremantle, noted this change from standard procedure, recalling: 'I remarked that it would be a good thing for them if on this occasion they had cavalry to follow up the broken infantry in the event of their succeeding in beating them. But to my surprise they all spoke of their cavalry as not efficient for that purpose. In fact, Stuart's men, though excellent at making raids, capturing wagons and stores, and cutting off communications, seem to have no idea of charging infantry under any circumstances.'

A 0.44-calibre Colt Army Model 1860 and below it a 0.36-calibre Colt Navy Model 1851 .

A visiting Austrian cavalry officer, Fitzgerald Ross, noted that Lee's use of cavalry was quite different from that practised in Europe: 'They are, in fact, mounted

infantry … there has been no time to put them through a regular cavalry drill, and teach the efficient use of the sabre – the true arm of real cavalry – whilst with the use of the rifle they have been familiar from their earliest youth. To handle a rifle efficiently, of course a man must dismount … Besides, the country is so wooded and broken up with high fences that opportunities for a regular cavalry-charge on a large scale seldom occur.'

Lee also ignored Jomini's suggestion that cavalry could not defend a position against infantry, sending Stuart south to block Grant's moves again and again in the 1864 campaign from the Wilderness to Petersburg. In these moves, however, they served as mounted infantry, riding to the threatened point, then dismounting and fighting on foot.

Lee expressed concern about his cavalry in a letter to Davis dated 5 July 1864, in which he said: 'The enemy is numerically superior to us in this arm, and possesses greater facilities for recruiting his horses and keeping them in serviceable condition. In the several engagements that have taken place between the cavalry of the two armies, I think great loss has been inflicted upon him, but it has been attended with a diminution of our force which we were less able to bear. Could I sweep his cavalry from the field, or preserve a fair proportion between its numbers and our own, I should feel that our present situation was in a measure secure. But in view of the disparity that exists, and the difficulty of increasing or even maintaining our force, I cannot but entertain serious apprehensions about the safety of our southern communications.' Lee was seeking reinforcements that Davis was largely unable to supply.

Lee was a master of logistics and the importance of keeping his men well clothed, fed, and equipped, and he was well aware of the high cost of mounted units. Horses had to be shoed, watered, and fed. A company of 85 cavalrymen, together with their 30 additional mules and pack horses used to haul company supplies, required 31,050 pounds of grain a month in summer, when they could graze, and 44,850 pounds in the winter. This placed a strain on a wholly inadequate transportation system that could barely keep up with the needs of his infantry. He was therefore forced to choose between infantry and cavalry, and chose at times, especially in winter quarters, to send his cavalry some distance away from the main army where it could be better supplied.

Problems of supplying horses also greatly affected Lee's use of artillery, whose organisation he tended to leave in the hands of his chief of artillery, William Pendleton. On 22 June 1862, Lee authorised the organisation Pendleton suggested, in which batteries assigned to brigades were directly under brigade commanders, while divisional reserve batteries reported to a divisional chief of artillery, each divisional chief reporting to Pendleton. Longstreet's Corps had five battalions and Jackson's had four; an additional battalion was assigned to each corps after the success of Confederate artillery at the Second Manassas. Pendleton was also responsible for field use of a general army reserve made up of artillery battalions.

This was a system that was advanced from the Federal artillery organisation of the time in that it allowed divisional chiefs and the army's reserve to concentrate their fire for maximum effort, rather than having guns played out all along a line by brigades. However, it hardly compensated for the fact that Confederate artillery, ammunition, and even friction primers were inferior to their Northern-made counterparts. Fuses were so bad that Confederate infantry would not allow their artillery to fire over their heads in support because of the frequent premature explosions. Moreover, many of the first guns brought into service were obsolete iron 6-pounders that lacked the range and power of the enemy's 12- and 10-pounders. Lee was well aware of this deficiency, writing to the Secretary of War on 5 December 1862: 'I am greatly in need of longer range smooth-bore guns, and propose that, if metal cannot otherwise be procured, a portion, if not all, of our 6-pounder smoothbores (bronze), and, if necessary, a part of our 12-pounder howitzers, be recast into 12-pounder Napoleons … The contest between our 6-pounder smoothbores and the 12-pounder Napoleons of the enemy is very unequal, and, in addition, is discouraging to our artillerists.'

Because of a lack of adequate guns, and problems in horse supply, Pendleton recommended, and Lee agreed to, a reduction in the number of field batteries

Lee's artillery chief throughout the war was William Nelson Pendleton. A priest for most of his life, despite an early U.S. Military Academy education, and older than most of Lee's officers, Pendleton's subordinates had no use for him and he was essentially relegated to paperwork for much of the war.

in the army in October 1862. In all, nineteen batteries were eliminated, their best men and guns being assigned to duty with consolidated batteries.

The 53-year-old Pendleton, however favoured by Lee, was considered a failure as a reserve artillery commander, unable to be active enough in the field, by his subordinates. Battalion commander Alexander thought that, 'He was too old & had been too long out of army life to be thoroughly up to all the opportunities of his position.' Lee was aware of this, but rather than hurt the feelings of his friend Pendleton, when he reorganised the army after Jackson's death, he divided all the artillery among the three corps and abolished the general artillery reserve. Pendleton from then on would simply perform administrative functions.

Actually Alexander also criticised Lee's tactical artillery knowledge on at least one occasion. At Fredericksburg he was just completing the emplacement of his guns when he learned that Lee had inspected the line and said that the gun emplacements should have been further back on the hill. When Alexander joined him, Lee said, 'Ah, Colonel Alexander, just see what a mistake Captain Johnston has made here in the location of his gun pits, putting them forward at the brow of the hill.' Alexander replied that the location was his order since from where they were they could 'see all this canister & short range ground … Back on the hill they can see nothing this side [of] the river.' Lee disagreed, saying that the position cost them range and ordering a change.

In fact, when the Federals finally charged the position, Alexander smugly noted, 'the guns there never fired a shot at their distant view, but thousands of rounds into infantry swarming over the canister & short range ground, & contributed greatly to the enemy's bloody repulse.' From then on Alexander frequently found himself in charge of locating gun positions.

On 23 April 1862, the Confederate high command authorised the recruitment of 'partisan rangers', who would serve in units behind enemy lines. If their activities had been co-ordinated with those of the main army, they could have been very useful in forcing the Federal forces to leave garrisons all along their lines of communications and supply, thereby weakening their main force. Moreover, they could have furnished intelligence, and harassed the enemy when Lee led his army on his raids into the North. Lee did not take advantage of this potential weapon, which was especially unfortunate when Stuart disappeared with the bulk of Lee's cavalry, removing the army's eyes. Lee could have used the rangers commanded by Major John S. Mosby, whom Stuart personally knew and depended on a great deal, to fill this gap, but he failed to do so.

Lee frankly distrusted partisan rangers. He even wrote to Richmond about the best of such units, Mosby's Rangers, then operating in northern Virginia: 'I fear he exercises but little control over his men. He has latterly carried but too few on his expeditions, apparently, and his attention has been more directed toward the capture of wagons than military damage to the enemy.' Indeed, on 3 April 1864, when the Secretary of War reacted to general complaints about the lack of discipline among ranger units, Lee, when asked for his opinion, wrote: 'Experience has convinced me that it is almost impossible, under the best officers even, to have discipline in these bands of Partisan Rangers, or to prevent them from becoming an injury instead of a benefit to the service, and even where this is accomplished the system gives license to many deserters & marauders, who assume to belong to these authorised companies & commit depredations on friend and foe alike … I hope the order will be issued at once disbanding the companies & battalions serving in this department.'

One of the great advantages the Army of the Potomac had over the Army of Northern Virginia, especially in the 1864 campaign, was its brigade of trained,

Rebel battery – a photograph attributed to J. D. Edwards. (US Corps of Engineers)

professional engineers. These men could rapidly throw bridges across Virginia's many rivers, which allowed the combat troops to keep up a rapid pace of march, then dismantle them and move up to the head of the column. They could build roads. Their topographical engineers could make and mass-produce maps to ensure that all commanders were in tune.

In his army Lee depended on a handful of professional officers in the Army's Corps of Engineers to supervise men detailed from the infantry as required to do the same sort of work. Of course, unit commanders took advantage of these details to get rid of their most worthless soldiers. For example, John O. Casler, a

deserter from the Stonewall Brigade, was returned to the army and in February 1863 was detailed, as punishment, to this 'Pioneer Corps'. He 'did not want to belong to it, for, on the march, we had to go in front of the division and carry our shovels, picks and axes, and repair the roads and bridges when necessary; and when a fight came off we had to go into the fight with a battery of artillery to cut out roads for them in the woods, or cut down timber in front that obstructed their view of the enemy, and remove blockades, etc … so it was all work and danger and no play …' Obviously such unwilling non-professionals would not do as good a job as regular trained engineers.

The Confederate Congress recognised this, and on 20 March 1863 authorised the organisation of regular regiments of engineers 'chosen with a view to their mechanical skill and physical fitness'. This was another system advance that Lee opposed. Although a full regiment and part of another were destined for his army, he had orders issued on 17 July 1863 'suspending' the formation of such units, any men already recruited to be 'returned to their companies'. Lee wrote to the Secretary of War giving an explanation for this suspension, stating that he disliked specialised units whose operations would be limited to specific engineering duties, especially if men to fill the units were taken from line units.

This time Lee was overruled. On 25 July the Secretary of War simply shot down Lee's objections, ordering him to accept the First Regiment of Engineer Troops under the command of his Army of Northern Virginia staff engineer, Major T. M. R. Talcott. Lee had no choice but to accept this innovation, but he was clearly displeased. However, he did make sure that, as Major William Blackford of the regiment recalled, the unit was 'armed and drilled as infantry, and in campaigns served as infantry unless there were military bridges or other works to construct'.

Officers of 69th New York Infantry at Fort Corcoran, Va. (Mathew Brady Collection)

LEE AND HIS OPPONENTS

Lee was in an unusual situation in that he had met all his opponents at one time or another in his pre-war military career, mostly through Mexican War service. Some of them, such as George McClellan, he knew well. Others, such as U. S. Grant, he had met only briefly and couldn't remember in later years.

His first major opponent, both in West Virginia and later when he first gained command of the Army of Northern Virginia outside Richmond was Major General George B. McClellan with whom he had worked closely in setting up artillery batteries when both were engineer officers during the Mexican War.

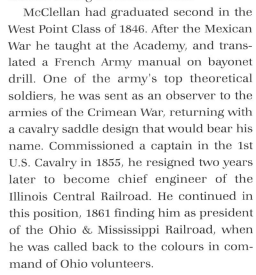

McClellan had graduated second in the West Point Class of 1846. After the Mexican War he taught at the Academy, and translated a French Army manual on bayonet drill. One of the army's top theoretical soldiers, he was sent as an observer to the armies of the Crimean War, returning with a cavalry saddle design that would bear his name. Commissioned a captain in the 1st U.S. Cavalry in 1855, he resigned two years later to become chief engineer of the Illinois Central Railroad. He continued in this position, 1861 finding him as president of the Ohio & Mississippi Railroad, when he was called back to the colours in command of Ohio volunteers.

McClellan, who had worked on the batteries in front of Mexico City with him, wrote to Abraham Lincoln on 20 April 1862, when he learned that Lee was in command of the force facing him, that: 'Lee is *too* cautious & weak under grave responsibility – personally brave & energetic to a fault, he yet is wanting in moral firmness when pressed by heavy responsibility & is likely to be timid & irresolute in action.' McClellan's total misreading of Lee's character is interesting and shows McClellan's own tendency to project his own inadequacies on to others.

Lee's first opponent was George McClellan, whom he totally understood and therefore did not fear at all. (Library of Congress)

In the Civil War it was McClellan, not Lee, who would prove to be 'timid & irresolute' in action, on top of which McClellan was not shown to be 'personally brave.' Indeed, Lee based much of his thinking about invading the North in 1862 on his understanding of McClellan's timidity. This was a widespread understanding after the Seven Days. Alexander felt that: 'Nobody in Lee's army was surprised then, & still less should anyone be surprised now when McClellan's inability to fight an army stands out so clearly in the light of his whole career, & particularly in his Sharpsburg campaign.'

Indeed, McClellan should have beaten Lee at Sharpsburg, having brought many more troops on to the field against Lee's divided army. Only his lack of field control that allowed his corps commanders to attack piecemeal enabled Lee to counter each attack in turn. Earlier Lee shook McClellan by attacking with such ferocity in the Seven Days, to the point where he simply knew that McClellan was overawed and would not continue to press towards Richmond. When he turned to confront Pope, Lee felt safe in leaving a small force to hold McClellan's much larger force.

Confederate Moxley Sorrel summed-up contemporary opinion that has largely survived to this day: 'McClellan was of decided ability in many respects; timorous, but safe; and there was no better organiser. He seemed to hate battle, and it is surprising that with such a record he should have secured and retained the devotion and confidence of his men to the very end. There was no lack of physical courage; it was a mental doubt about him.' Modern historians have modified this to suggest that there may well have been a 'lack of physical courage' in McClellan as well.

While his soldiers liked and trusted McClellan, his actions, or lack of them, cost him dearly in term of public and political support. The *New York Times* reporter William Swinton, who covered the Army of the Potomac, wrote after the war that McClellan 'had already put the patience of the public and Administration to a severe strain by his six months' inactivity; and in his proposal to remove his army from the front of Washington [for the Peninsula campaign], he made another and peculiarly heavy draft upon their confidence. In this he again exposed himself to the criticism already made respecting his deficiency in those statesmanlike qualities that enter into the composition of a great general.'

Yet Lee found McClellan to be the general he most respected. Field Marshal Viscount Wolseley later recalled, 'Lee mentioned McClellan with most respect and regard.' Given their similar backgrounds and experience, Lee obviously felt it an advantage that his opponent was McClellan. 'I am sorry to part with General McClellan,' he said, when he learned that McClellan had been replaced as commander of the Army of the Potomac in 1862, 'for we have come to understand each other so well. I am afraid, if they continue to make these changes, they will find some one whom I don't understand.' Lee certainly understood McClellan, and was only surprised by him on one occasion, this being the rapidity

The opponent Lee disdained the most was John Pope, shown here from a *Harper's Weekly* engraving from a photograph. He made quick work of him at Second Manassas, although Lee's victory could have been greater had he forced Longstreet to be more aggressive.

of his movements at Sharpsburg, but when he learned that his orders had fallen into the hands of the Union general, everything fell into place.

Lee was not to respect his next opponent, John Pope, at all. Pope had graduated from West Point in 1852, and he too had served as an engineer in the Mexican War. There he won brevet commissions of first lieutenant and captain. He remained in the army after the war, his most recent commission to captain of Topographical Engineers coming in 1856. Serving in the west, he led forces that opened the upper Mississippi River, capturing Madrid and Island No. 10. He was promoted to major general of volunteers on 22 March 1862. As Lincoln clearly saw that McClellan's Peninsula Campaign was drawing to an end, he brought Pope east to face Lee, in command of an army made up of units in the Washington area.

Those who actually met and dealt with Pope were impressed by him. Colonel David Strother, who met him in June 1862, wrote: 'Pope is a bright, dashing man, self-confident and clearheaded. He has a good memory and has been a topographical engineer. I observe that he is wonderfully quick to seize all information on this subject. He remembers it all if once told and wants new details. Whether his mind grasps general subjects with capacity and clearness I have not had an opportunity to judge. He is irascible and impulsive in his judgements of men, but in his pleasant moods, jolly, humorous, and clever in conversation.'

On the other side of the front lines, Sorrel recalled that Pope: 'was a man of some ability, but did not have a reputation for high character in the old Army; and now with elevated rank and command thrust upon him, he turned to abuse of his enemy, explained how he meant to whip him, and filled the air with bombast and threatening. He was in command in northern Virginia, and Lee had marked him for his own.'

Pope was a total failure. He issued orders that apparently denigrated the fighting abilities of Union soldiers in the east, and alienated his own men. He issued harsh orders concerning quartering his troops on the land and punishing those civilians believed to be in sympathy or aiding the Confederates. He blamed others for all his own misjudgements, especially Army of the Potomac corps commander Fitz-John Porter. His getting the popular Porter court-martialled and relieved of duty cost him the favour of the officer corps. Finally, he allowed himself to be totally confused by Lee's and Jackson's moves at the Second Manassas and evaded total destruction of his army only by his men's hard fighting and a bit of luck when Longstreet failed to move aggressively enough against him.

Pope was the sole Union army opponent towards whom Lee felt vindictive. He detested the man, writing to Jackson on 27 July 1862, 'I want Pope to be suppressed. The course indicated in his orders if the newspapers report them correctly cannot be permitted and will lead to retaliation on our part.'

He clearly understood McClellan's successor in command of the Army of the Potomac, Ambrose Burnside. Alexander noted, when Burnside replaced McClellan, that 'Burnside did not want the position, but took it with the advice of

Everyone liked Ambrose Burnside, Lee's next opponent. His tactical and strategic abilities, however, were considerably less than his social skills.

his friends, to keep it from being offered to Hooker; of whom the old army … by no means approved. Burnside was a man almost universally popular, though few thought him, & he did not apparently think himself, any great general. In my mind his name is associated with "Benny Havens's" [public house] near West Point, for he was old Benny's greatest admiration of all cadets ever at the Academy. He had graduated long before me, & had left the army but old Benny was always talking, even in my day, of "Ambrose Burnside".'

After West Point Burnside went into the artillery and served mostly on garrison duties during the Mexican War. He resigned his commission in 1853 to set up a plant to make a breech-loading carbine which he designed and hoped to sell to the army. The business failed, and thereafter he was elected to a term in the U.S. Congress, finally getting a job under McClellan in the Illinois Central Railroad. When the war broke out he organised the 1st Rhode Island Infantry, which he brought to the Army of the Potomac where he was quickly named a brigade commander.

Officers and men in the Army of the Potomac, which essentially McClellan had created, were quite unhappy to see Burnside replace their favourite general. Soon afterwards, the army's Provost-General, Marsena Patrick wrote, 'He appeared well – very well, but all seemed to think there was one they liked much better.' Patrick added that he felt Burnside was 'rather obtuse in his conceptions & is very forgetful.' After Burnside was replaced, Patrick noted that, 'He is unfit for a separate command.'

U. S. Grant, to whom Burnside directly reported in the 1864 campaign, later wrote that: 'General Burnside was an officer who was generally liked and respected. He was not, however, fitted to command an army. No one knew this better than himself. He always admitted his blunders, and extenuated those officers under him beyond what they were entitled to. It was hardly his fault that he was ever assigned to a separate command.'

Swinton felt that Burnside's performance was hindered since he 'unfeignedly regarded [McClellan] as his superior in ability … To the public his modest shrinking and solicitude appeared the sign of a noble nature, wronging itself in its proper estimate, and it was adjudged that he was a man of such temper that the exercise of great trusts would presently bring him a sense of confidence and power. And, indeed, severely just though Burnside's judgement of his own capacity afterwards proved, there was at the moment no man who seemed so well fitted to succeed McClellan. Of the other corps commanders of the Army of the Potomac, no one had proved his capacity in the exercise of independent command. But Burnside, as chief of the North Carolina expedition, brought the prestige of a successful perseverance, and above all, a high degree of patriotic zeal. Frank, manly, and generous in character, he was beloved by his own corps, and respected by the army generally.'

Across the front lines, Sorrel recalled that: 'Burnside had no prominent reputation, but made a success of an unimportant expedition into North Carolina [in early 1862]. He conspicuously failed at Sharpsburg, where all day the bridge on the right was the scene of combat, without his movement to seize it. His great corps, held idly in hand, was equal to it ten times over. But he may have been waiting on McClellan, with whom he was in the closest intimacy of friendship. At all events, Burnside could and would fight, even if he did not know how, and after "Little Mac" this was what Mr. Lincoln was trying for.'

But Burnside's attempts to fight failed, and he had to go. He would be replaced by Joseph Hooker.

Hooker was a graduate from the West Point Class of 1837. He served on a divisional commander's staff during the Mexican War, winning brevets through to the rank of lieutenant colonel for his service there. Although commissioned into the artillery, after the Mexican War he remained on staff duties, serving as assistant adjutant-general of the Pacific Division. While there he resigned his commission to take up farming in Sonoma, California, in 1853. On his return to the east coast, he re-entered the army as a brigadier general of volunteers on 6 August1862.

He commanded a division in the Peninsula campaign during which time a newspaper article headlined an article 'Fighting – Joe Hooker', and this became his nickname, much to his personal disgust. Promoted to major general thereafter, he was given command of the Army of the Potomac's I Corps and then the 'Centre Grand Division' of two corps at Fredericksburg.

Hooker was not of sterling character. Grant commanded him at Chattanooga where he said 'his achievement in bringing his command around the point of Lookout Mountain and into Chattanooga Valley was brilliant. I nevertheless regarded him as a dangerous man. He was not subordinate to his superiors. He was ambitious to the extent of caring nothing for the rights of others. His disposition was, when engaged in battle, to get detached from the main body of the army and exercise a separate command, gathering to his standard all he could of his juniors.'

Burnside was one of Hooker's targets, and the latter general actively plotted behind his then commander's back to replace him. Burnside was aware of this, and towards the end of his service as army commander filed charges against Hooker for 'unjust and unnecessary criticism of the actions of his superior officers, and of the authorities, and having by the general tone of his conversations endeavoured to create distrust in the minds of officers who have associated with him, and having, by omissions and otherwise, made reports and statements which were calculated to create incorrect impressions, and for habitually speaking in disparaging terms of other officers …'

The public was unaware of all this, seeing only, as Swinton wrote, that as a corps commander, 'he won the reputation of being what is called a "dashing" officer, and earned the sobriquet of "Fighting Joe". He had gained great popularity both in the army and throughout the country – a result to which his fine soldierly appearance and frank manners had much contributed; nor was this diminished by a habit he had of self-assertion, which, however, proved little, since it may be either the manifestation of important conceit, or the proud utterance of conscious power.'

Hooker did not fool Lincoln, who still had few choices in replacing Burnside. On 26 January 1863, Lincoln wrote to tell him that he had placed him in charge because he felt that he could do a good job. But he warned him that he was aware, 'that during General Burnside's command of the army you have taken counsel of your ambition, and thwarted him as much as you could, in which you did a great wrong to the country and to a most meritorious and honourable brother officer.' He added that he heard that Hooker was in favour of a military dictator replacing the president, and noted that only successful generals could

Lee called Joseph Hooker, his opponent at Chancellorsville, 'Mr. F. J. Hooker', after the Union general's nickname of 'Fighting Joe'.

become dictators. 'What I now ask of you is military success, and I will risk the dictatorship,' he wrote.

Hooker was smart enough not to dash his army immediately towards Richmond, but instead took time to rebuild a badly shaken force. He arranged for furloughs. He got decent and plentiful rations to the men, getting them fresh bread four times a week and fresh vegetables twice. He cut desertion by stopping civilians from shipping civilian clothing to the troops so that they could escape, while at the same time having deserters quickly arrested and shot. He made major changes in the medical department that improved sanitary conditions and cut sickness. He gathered the army's scattered cavalry units, that were being wasted in tasks such as courier and guard service, and brought them into one corps. Under him the cavalry would finally become the equal of Lee's. He created an intelligence unit that finally produced good information on Confederate organisations and numbers. He even took an idea first used by a divisional commander, a system of unique badges which identified each wearer and corps, established army-wide. This proved an invaluable morale builder. Finally, he came up with an excellent plan to attack and beat Lee's army, a plan that would take his troops to Chancellorsville.

In short, 'Fighting Joe Hooker' was a fine general as 'Administrative Joe Hooker'. But his fighting qualities at Chancellorsville did not match his previous actions. He was decisively beaten there, having finally lost his nerve. He was not immediately replaced as the army's commander, as Lee began his thrust into Pennsylvania. He began moving his army north to follow Lee while shielding Washington. As part of his defence against Lee, he requested the Harpers Ferry garrison to be reinforced. The Union Army's General-in-Chief Henry Halleck forbade this, and Hooker submitted his resignation. To his apparent surprise it was accepted, and he was relieved.

Lee, who based part of his plan on invading Pennsylvania on the demoralisation of Hooker, whom he condescendingly called 'Mr. F. J. Hooker' in private, could not have been happy to learn on the eve of Gettysburg, that he was no longer in command.

Lincoln now asked Major General Darius Couch, who commanded a corps at Chancellorsville, taking over Hooker's job when he was put out of action, to take the army's command. Never a well man, Couch declined for health reasons, instead taking command of troops in Pennsylvania. Couch suggested another corps commander, George Gordon Meade, for the job.

Meade was born in Spain in 1815 to a Pennsylvania native who had lost his fortune during the Napoleonic Wars. Appointed to West Point, he graduated 19th in the 56-man-strong Class of 1835. Not especially interested in a military career, he resigned his commission a year later to take up civil engineering. However, in 1842 he returned to the army as a second lieutenant in the Corps of Topographical Engineers. He was breveted a first lieutenant in the Mexican War. He was a captain in the corps at the outbreak of the Civil War when the Governor of Pennsylvania, Andrew Curtin, had him appointed brigadier general of volunteers and gave him command of a brigade of the state's troops. Badly wounded in the Seven Days campaign, he returned to command at the Second Manassas and had a division's command at Sharpsburg. After Fredericksburg, where his troops achieved some of the few Union successes in the battle, he was chosen to command the V Corps. He was appointed commander of the Army of the Potomac on 28 June 1863, and would command that force until Lee's surrender.

On learning of Meade's appointment on the eve of the Battle of Gettysburg, Lee indicated that he thought Meade was a better general than Hooker. He is reported to have said that, 'General Meade will commit no blunder on my front, and if I make one he will make haste to take advantage of it.'

Meade did not make any blunder, but neither did he perform as Lincoln wanted. In Washington the politicians felt that Meade let Lee escape relatively unharmed back into Virginia after Gettysburg much as McClellan had done after Sharpsburg. Meade was aware of this, and moved more rapidly in a series of manoeuvres in the Bristoe Station and Mine Run Campaigns. But neither general ever felt comfortable enough to actually commit themselves to a major battle in these late 1863 campaigns. When Meade agreed to call off a planned attack at Mine Run he felt that it would be the end of his career, since he was very much aware of Lincoln's desire to bring Lee to battle. But he felt that such an attack would have been a Fredericksburg-like disaster, and the high command kept him in his post.

Lincoln did, however, bring the successful western general Ulysses S. Grant to Washington to oversee the entire Union army's war effort. Grant decided not to remain in that city, directing movements across the country by telegraph, and actually accompanied Meade's Army of the Potomac in its campaign against Lee's army in 1865. Moreover, he would have Burnside's independent command report directly to him, rather than Meade, as an equal to Meade even though the command was serving hand-in-glove with the Army of the Potomac. Such a command structure was bound to be uncomfortable for Meade.

The result was that blame for such disasters as the assault at Cold Harbor fell to Grant, but so too did praise for the eventual victory. Meade fell into the background and felt thereafter that his role in the eventual victory had been unfairly ignored.

Grant, however, was more than generous in praising Meade. On 13 May 1864, from the front at Spotsylvania Court House, he wrote to the Secretary of War: 'General Meade has more than met my most sanguine expectations. He and Sherman are the fittest officers for large commands I have ever come in contact with.'

George Gordon Meade was nominated to command the Army of the Potomac after Hooker's resignation and would lead it until Lee's eventual surrender at Appomattox.

After the war Grant in his memoirs summed-up his view of Meade: 'General Meade was an officer of great merit, with drawbacks to his usefulness that were beyond his control. He had been an officer of the engineer corps before the war, and consequently had never served with troops until he was over forty-six years of age. He never had, I believe, a command of less than a brigade. He saw clearly and distinctly the position of the enemy, and the topography of the country in front of his own position. His first idea was to take advantage of the lay of the ground, sometimes without reference to the direction we wanted to move afterwards. He was subordinate to his superiors in rank to the extent that he could execute an order which changed his own plans with the same zeal he would have displayed if the plan had been his own. He was brave and conscientious, and commanded the respect of all who knew him. He was unfortunately of a temper that would get beyond his control, at times, and make him speak to officers of high rank in the most offensive manner. No one saw this fault more plainly than he himself, and no one regretted it more. This made it unpleasant at times, even in battle, for those around him to approach him even with information. In spite of this defect he was a most valuable officer and deserves a high place in the annals of his country.'

In fact, however, it was Grant who planned the strategy and directed the tactical movements in the final campaign against Lee.

Grant had largely been a failure in life before the war. Born in Ohio in 1822, his father got him into West Point in 1839. He disliked military life so much there that he hoped that Congress would close the academy, something which was being debated at the time. His horsemanship was outstanding, but he was posted to the infantry after graduating twenty-first in the 39-man-strong Class of 1843.

A regimental staff officer in the Mexican War, he served with distinction and valour, earning brevets to first lieutenant and captain, under Zachary Taylor, who was noted for his informal appearance and attitude, which probably influenced Grant's lack of pomp when in command. Posted to the Pacific Northwest after the war and separated from a wife whom he dearly loved and depended on, he apparently began drinking. He resigned his commission in 1854 before any charges could be brought because of that.

The next years were hard for Grant and his family. He failed at farming, selling real estate, and clerking in a customs-house. He finally had to go to work in his brother's leather store in Galena, Illinois, where he was when the Civil War broke out. He tried to get a commission at that point, hopefully as a brigadier general of volunteers, but was ignored until 17 June 1861, when he was nominated colonel of the 21st Illinois Infantry. On 7 August 1861 he was appointed as a brigadier general of volunteers.

From the start, Grant stood out among Union generals as being aggressive, bringing the war to the South immediately and constantly. After surviving a failed attack at Beaumont, Missouri, he brought his forces to the Confederates' Forts Henry and Donelson, and took them both. His demand for an unconditional surrender of Donelson brought him the popular nickname 'Unconditional Surrender', and a promotion to major general of volunteers. Grant was uninterested in his opponents' plans; he simply ignored them while he concentrated on what he wanted to do. This attitude almost brought him disaster at Shiloh when a Confederate force smashed into his unprepared troops. Strong reinforcements arrived in the evening of the battle's first day, and the opposing Confederate general, Albert Sidney Johnston, was mortally wounded. Grant was therefore able to return to the attack next day, forcing the Confederates to retreat to their original base at Corinth.

Henry Halleck, the overall theatre commander, thereafter took over command from Grant, who almost resigned rather than continue as second-in-command. Instead, after Corinth's capture, Grant concerned himself with capturing the stronghold of Vicksburg on the Mississippi River. His first attempt was a failure, and he changed his plans to pass the city by boat, land south of the city and then take it from that direction. At the same time he sent troops east to stop any Confederate attempts to relieve the city from that direction. Attempts to take the city by attack failed and he settled in for a siege. On 4 July 1863, Vicksburg surrendered, a one-two punch against the Confederacy, coming a day after the last day at Gettysburg.

Promoted to major general in the regular U.S. Army for this success, he was then brought to command troops besieged in Chattanooga. Aided by reinforcements, including two corps under Hooker, he broke the siege and drove the Confederates southwards. He was then made a lieutenant general, the first since George Washington, and given command of all the Union armies.

In this role Grant proved to have the best strategic abilities of any Civil War general. He planned a co-ordinated assault everywhere against the Confederacy, with one army driving towards Atlanta, one landing south of Richmond and driving through Petersburg to that city, one heading south through the Valley of Virginia, while other forces took Mobile, Alabama. The Army of the Potomac would aim at destroying the Army of Virginia in the east, and Grant chose to accompany this force personally.

General Ulysses S. Grant at Cold Harbor, 1864. (Mathew Brady Collection)

Like Lee, Grant felt it was an advantage to have known an opponent in that war, since, he later wrote: 'The natural disposition of most people is to clothe a commander of a large army whom they do not know, with almost superhuman abilities. A large part of the National army, for instance, and most of the press of the country, clothed General Lee with just such qualities, but I had known him personally, and knew that he was mortal; and it was just as well that I felt this.'

As a result, Grant never lost his nerve as Hooker did. He forced Lee to react to his moves and simply did not stop until his job was done. He refused to allow Lee to have that freedom of manoeuvre that Lee so much depended upon. The result was that once Grant took personal command, Lee, the Army of Northern Virginia, and the Confederacy itself were doomed.

HOW HISTORY VIEWS LEE

Scholarly history has not been kind to Robert E. Lee and his cause even though they both remain legends in popular culture. The Confederate cause, once accepted to have been an attempt to retain 18th-century values and government, is now generally seen as having been an attempt by an oligarchy to retain rule over the masses, voiding democracy and a popular will – mob rule, the Confederacy's founders would have called it.

Lee's status in history began while he was still creating it. His soldiers trusted and respected him beyond any other officer, except Jackson while he lived. John S. R. Miller, adjutant and company officer in the 1st North Carolina State Troops wrote to his mother on 10 June 1863, as the Army of Northern Virginia started on the road to Gettysburg: 'I scarcely think we will have a general engagement as the Yanks are disposed to play "shy" as they have been so roughly handled that they can scarcely make up their minds and when they do soon become [so] terror stricken that they show no courage or determination … Our troops are so accustomed to victory that it would be impossible to whip them. You need have no uneasiness about us at home as we're perfectly confident and with Lee to guide us are certain of success.'

Although some troops changed their opinion of Lee as a wholly perfect general after the charge of 3 July at Gettysburg, on the whole he retained the trust of his army through to the final surrender. Indeed, most of Lee's lower ranking soldiers were astonished by the surrender, being sure that Lee, now free to manoeuvre, would get them out of harm's way and unite with Johnston's forces in North Carolina.

So Lee left command honoured by both sides, despite having surrendered his army in the field. Even Grant, who was not easily impressed, described Lee at Appomattox as being 'handsomely dressed, six feet high and of faultless form'. In the conversation at the surrender itself, Grant recalled telling Lee 'that there was not a man in the Confederacy whose influence with the soldiery and the whole people was as great as his …'

Lee's attitude thereafter, one of no apparent bitterness, and of reconciliation with the victors, brought him praise on both sides of the Mason–Dixon Line. Coloured engravings of Lee, often at his last meeting with Jackson at Chancellorsville, soon appeared in parlours throughout the South.

After the war Richard Taylor, son of the victorious Mexican War general and himself a general under Lee in 1862, wrote: 'Of all the men I have seen, he was best entitled to the epithet of distinguished; and so marked was his appearance in this particular, that he would not have passed unnoticed through the streets of any capital. Reserved almost to coldness, his calm dignity repelled familiarity; not that he seemed without sympathies, but that he had so conquered his own

Lee was photo-
graphed after the war
in his usual field
uniform and on his
favourite horse,
Traveller.

weaknesses as to prevent the confession of others before him … Yet his lofty
character was respected of all and compelled public confidence. Indeed, his
character seemed perfect, his bath in Stygian waters complete; not a vulnerable
spot remained: *totus teres atque rotundus*. His soldiers reverenced him and had
unbounded confidence in him, for he shared all their privations, and they saw
him ever unshaken of fortune. Tender and protecting love he did not inspire:
such love is given to weakness, not to strength. Not only was he destitute of a
vulgar greed for fame, he would not extend a hand to welcome it when it came
unbidden. He was without ambition, and, like Washington, into whose family
connection he had married, kept duty as his guide.

'His wonderful defensive campaign in 1864 stands with that of Napoleon in
1813; and the comparison only fails by an absence of sharp returns to the offensive
… in truth the genius of Lee for offensive war had suffered by a too long service
as an engineer … In both the Antietam and Gettysburg campaigns he allowed his
cavalry to separate from him, and was left without intelligence of the enemy's
movements until he was upon him. In both, too, his army was widely scattered,
and had to be brought into action by piecemeal … His own report of Gettysburg
confesses his mistakes; for he was of too lofty a nature to seek scapegoats …
Nevertheless, from the moment Lee succeeded to the command of the army in

Virginia, he was *facile princeps* in the war, towering above all on both sides, as the pyramid of Ghizeh above the desert ... Last scene of all, at his surrender, his greatness and dignity made of his adversary but a humble accessory; and if departed intelligences be permitted to take ken of the affairs of the world, the soul of Light Horse Harry rejoices in his own eulogy of Washington, "First in war, first in peace, first in the hearts of his countrymen", is now, by the united voice of the South, applied to his noble son.'

As with Taylor, observers admired two different aspects of Lee: Lee the gentleman and Lee the warrior.

As to Lee the gentleman, all agreed he was essentially the finest example known to this day of what a Southerner of good breeding and behaviour should be. British Field Marshal Viscount Wolseley, who visited Lee's headquarters in late 1862, subsequently wrote: 'General Lee's presence commanded respect, even from strangers, by a calm self-possessed dignity, the like of which I have never seen in other men. Naturally of strong passions, he kept them under perfect control by that iron and determined will, of which his expression and his face gave evidence. As this tall, handsome soldier stood before his countrymen, he was the picture of the ideal patriot, unconscious and self-possessed in his strength: he indulged in no theatrical display of feeling: there was in his face and about him that placid resolve which bespoke great confidence in his self, and which in his case – one knows not how – quickly communicated its magnetic influence to others.' While Taylor found him obviously somewhat off-putting, as any such Eastern-raised Southerner might appear to someone from the more rough-and-tumble west, most people found him visually impressive, quick to put them at ease, and probably the most impressive individual they had ever seen.

In terms of Lee the warrior, war-time comrades were the first to create a myth of the 'perfect' general because of his military abilities, ignoring such few failings as Taylor suggested, as well as his social graces. Of these the most notable was Jubal Early. In his address to Washington and Lee University in 1872, Early opined that 'very few, comparatively, have formed a really correct estimate of his marvellous ability and boldness as a military commander, however exalted is the merit generally awarded him in that respect.' Early set out to correct that mistake through speeches, publications, and squashing any opposition to Lee's perfect record by contemporaries, especially Longstreet. Longstreet, in effect, became the Trotsky of Confederate military history in the view of many contemporary ex-Confederate soldiers for his acceptance of Federal victory and public disagreement with Lee's tactics, especially at Gettysburg.

A young adult's biography of Lee, *The Life of General Robert E. Lee* by Mary Williamson, published in 1895, was typical of what ordinary Americans were told about the general. She wrote that Lee only surrendered because 'he had to give up at last because he had no more men and no more food', claiming outlandishly that Lee had only 8,000 men then facing Grant's 200,000. Williamson added that, 'Perhaps no man ever lived that was so great, so good, and so unselfish as Lee.'

The traditional views of Lee, enlarged by post-war myth making, lasted well into the 20th century, culminating with Virginia historian Douglas Southall Freeman's epic of praise to the general, as written in his biography of 1934: 'In the dark period after the War between the States, the most glamorous memory of the South was that of the Confederate cause, whose finest figure was Lee. In his military achievement, Southern [white] people saw the flowering of their racial stock; in his social graces they behold their ideals embodied; in the honours paid his memory, every one of Lee's former soldiers felt that he had himself received the accolade.' Freeman's three-volume set became the standard work on the general and influenced historians for generations.

Lee's birthday was widely celebrated in the South. In 1901 he was nominated to the Hall of Fame. In 1928 the Robert E. Lee Memorial Foundation was formed to buy and restore his birthplace. His face later appeared on a postage stamp issued by the country he fought to destroy – only the first of several times it would so appear. Lee's name graced all sorts of public works, from highways to schools. Indeed, tiny Midland, Texas, so far from Lee's Virginia, named its high school the Robert E. Lee High School (the football team were naturally 'the Rebels').

The leading writer on Lee a generation after Freeman was another Virginian, Clifford Dowdey, who felt that Lee combined 'the harmony of the powerful elements in his nature which gave the quality of grandeur to his character'. He added that, 'There was a kinglike quality in his leadership, as if by divine right, and he was the product of a society that had trained its superior individuals for authority.' In terms of military ability, 'What he brought that changed the pattern of the armed struggle was strategy, the first introduced by the Confederates in their defence,' he wrote. 'Since this strategy was adapted to the administration's general policy of defence, Lee also brought to the war in Virginia the first instance in which the military objective perfectly expressed the political purposes.'

Conflicting views to this laudatory chorus sounded from time to time. Grant in 1878 remarked that, 'I never ranked Lee as high as some others of the army, that is to say, I never had as much anxiety when he was in my front as when Joe Johnston was in front.' After the war Union staff officer George Bruce suggested that Lee 'can never be placed in the ranks of those great captains who have affected the fortunes of nations, for good or ill, as commander of the national forces. In this respect he falls far below Washington and Grant.' He added that outside the Virginia theatre, 'Lee's influence with reference to the general affairs of the Confederacy was negative and accomplished absolutely nothing.' However, it was not until 1977 when Tennessee historian Thomas Connelly published his *The Marble Man, Robert E. Lee and His Image in American Society*, that attempts to bring Lee into a more balanced place in Civil War history began to affect mainstream thinking.

Connelly, noting that the majority of Southern citizens were more concerned with the war in the west than in Virginia, noted that 'until the last three months of the war, Lee commanded only a single Confederate army. Lee's surrender at Appomattox Court House has become synonymous with the end of the war, but his single army consisted of only 25,000 men, whereas some 100,000 Confederates remained under arms in major field forces in North Carolina, Alabama, and the trans-Mississippi region. Yet Lee has been depicted as the central figure of the Rebel populace, the man to whom all looked for salvation.' Connelly went on to say that, 'The image is one which contains both truth and distortion.'

Far from endorsing Dowdey's views, Connelly felt that, 'He had difficulty in grasping the relationship between war and statecraft and saw his responsibility as a commander of an army and little more.' Moreover, he wrote, 'His concept

A drawing by a British artist of Jackson's headquarters, which appeared in *Harper's Weekly*. This small collection of tents is quite similar to the headquarters set up by Lee whenever he halted.

of the war effort was almost totally identified with Virginia, and he felt that other theatres were secondary to the eastern front. While Lee's love for Virginia helped engender this parochialism, his personality was also responsible.'

Equally importantly, Connelly believed that, 'Lee's aggressive nature bled the Confederacy of manpower. In his first two years as commander of the Virginia army, Lee threw his men into combat in furious assaults. His offensive tactics were dreadfully expensive, and British historian Liddell Hart wrote that a wiser course might have to been to combine offensive strategy and defensive tactics, "to lure the Union armies into attacking under disadvantageous conditions ...".'

Connelly's book, tossing out totally the usual view of Lee, created a tremendous controversy. Traditionalists were appalled and leapt to Lee's defence. Army of Tennessee historian Richard McMurry retorted in *Two Great Rebel Armies*, 'Connelly's attacks on Lee for his personality and his battlefield successes are very weak ... It cannot be disputed that Lee enjoyed a great deal of success on the battlefield. Connelly, however, confuses cause and effect and ignores the extent to which Lee – unlike his western counterparts – was able, to a surprising degree, to shape the environment in which his army operated.' Moreover, he added, 'Lee's advice to give primacy to the war in Virginia reflected both his own conviction that the Old Dominion was the most important theatre of the conflict and the bureaucratic imperative that he preserve the strength of his own army.'

Despite traditionalist arguments, blows against Lee's reputation continued. Mid-western historian Alan T. Nolan, well known for his history of the Army of the Potomac's Iron Brigade, published his *Lee Considered, General Robert E. Lee and Civil War History*.

Nolan wrote that when Lee wrote about his thinking in 1861 he reflected 'a gift for self-delusion', adding, 'When all is said and done, it appears that Lee had an unusually high tolerance for ambiguous loyalty.' He noted that, 'It seems plain that the traditional premise – that the South simply could not have won the war – has had much to do with the establishing of Lee's reputation as an almost perfect general. Indeed, the entire direction of one's inquiry into Lee's generalship depends on whether one accepts the tradition of the inevitable loss of the Lost Cause or alternatively sees the success of that cause as a possibility.'

'Lee believed that the South's grand strategic role was offensive,' Nolan wrote. 'There was a profound problem with Lee's grand strategy of the offensive: it was not feasible to defeat the North militarily as distinguished from prolonging the contest until the North gave it up.'

Summing it up, Nolan felt that 'there were at least four aspects of Lee's own assessment of his army's situation that ran counter to the logic of his grand strategy of the offensive. He was aware of his numerical disadvantage, believed a siege would assure his defeat, and thought it critical for the South to keep its armies in the field. Yet his offensives consistently produced high casualty rates, and these casualties exacerbated the manpower differential, made a siege more likely, and reduced the Confederacy's ability to maintain an effective fighting force.'

Michael Marino wrote an article 'Attack and Destroy: Lee, Napoleon, and the Civil War,' that appeared in the Winter 1998 issue of the quarterly review *Columbiad*. In it Marino wrote of Lee: 'An analysis of his campaigns shows him to be an extremely conservative man, unwilling or unable to adapt to the many changes in warfare that had occurred by the time of the Civil War. Against all odds, he sought to destroy an enemy using methods that had worked for Napoleon years before. Unfortunately for the Confederate cause, his outdated tactics and stubborn refusal to adapt to new military developments cost the war.'

A dead Confederate sharpshooter, Gettysburg, July 1863, photographed by Alexander Gardner. (US War Dept.)

In 2000 Steven Newton indirectly attacked Lee's battlefield abilities in his study of strengths of the Confederate armies in 1864. Newton's findings suggested to him that in the campaign to Petersburg, 'Contrary to popular myth, from a manpower perspective the Confederates should be seen as the winners of the contest in May and June. By the time the lines had somewhat stabilised around Richmond and Petersburg, the Southerners still retained their original ratio of force to the Union army, even after the detachment of four small infantry divisions to the Shenandoah Valley without any corresponding Federal movement. Moreover, Lee received the bulk of his reinforcements in organised divisions and brigades, which could be employed as coherent units from their first hours, while Grant received a hodge-podge of individual regiments of varying size and quality which had to be integrated into shattered brigades of weary veterans before they could become truly combat effective. The result was that the Army of Northern Virginia enjoyed a tactical edge throughout the summer and early fall which nearly offset not just Grant's superiority of numbers but almost cancelled out the negative effects of several poor strategic/operational decisions in response to Federal offensives.'

These iconoclastic works were no more accepted by all Civil War historians than Connelly's had been. In 2001 Gary Gallagher, a university professor and frequent essayist and editor of collections of Civil War essays, took the other point of view, arguing 'against representations of Lee as either a glorious or misguided anachronism. Lee understood very well the kind of war in which he was engaged and what it took to win it.' Gallagher's opinion was that Lee 'crafted a strategy based on a careful, if sometimes flawed, reading of the military and political situation and ultimately saw his best efforts dissolve in absolute defeat.' Indeed, Gallagher saw even Lee as more of a Southern nationalist than a Virginian.

So the academic debate is likely to continue well into the future. In the popular mind, however, Lee is perhaps already fading from memory. In 1942, for example, the Virginia-based, 24-county-strong council of the Boy Scouts of America voted to name itself the 'Robert E. Lee Council'. In the spring of 2003, however, that same council voted to drop Lee's name, a spokesman noting that the name was considered by some 'an offensive relic of the past', although officially the council's spokesman said it simply wanted a name that would better reflect the geography the council covered.

SELECT BIBLIOGRAPHY

Alexander, Edward Porter. *Military Memoirs of a Confederate*. New York, 1993

Baylies, Francis. *A Narrative of Major General Wool's Campaign in Mexico in The Years 1846, 1847 & 1848*. Albany, New York, 1851

Beck, Brandon H. (ed.). *Third Alabama! The Civil War Memoir of Brigadier General Cullen Andrews Battle, CSA*. Tuscaloosa, Alabama, 2000

Bigelow, John, Jr. *Chancellorsville*. New York, 1995

Blackford, W. W. *War Years with Jeb Stuart*. New York, 1945

Casler, John O. *Four Years With The Stonewall Brigade*. Dayton, Ohio, 1994

Connelly, Thomas L. *The Marble Man: Robert E. Lee and His Image in American Society*. Baton Rouge, Louisiana, 1977

Crackel, Theodore J. *The Illustrated History of West Point*. West Point, New York, 1991

Crouch, Howard R. *Virginia Militaria of the Civil War*. Fairfax, Virginia, n.d.

Davis, Jefferson. *The Rise and Fall of the Confederate Government*. New York, 1881

Dowdey, Clifford. *The Seven Days: the Emergence of Robert E. Lee*. New York, 1978

Dowdey, Clifford, and Manarin, Louis H. (eds.). *The Wartime Papers of R. E. Lee*. New York, 1961

Early, Jubal A. *Narrative of the War Between the States*. New York, 1989

Eicher, David J. *Robert E. Lee, A Life Portrait*. New York, 1997

Freeman, Douglas Southall. *R. E. Lee*. New York, 1934

Furgurson, Ernest B. *Chancellorsville 1863: The Souls of the Brave*. New York, 1992

Gallagher, Gary W. (ed.). *Lee and His Army in Confederate History*. Chapel Hill, North Carolina, 20001

— *Chancellorsville: The Battle and its Aftermath*. Chapel Hill, North Carolina, 1996

— *Fighting for the Confederacy: The Personal Recollections of General Edward Porter Alexander*. Chapel Hill, North Carolina, 1989

— *Lee The Soldier*. Lincoln, Nebraska, 1996

Gordon, John B. *Reminiscences of the Civil War*. New York, 1903

Grant, U. S. *Personal Memoirs*. New York, 1952

Hennessy, John J. *Return to Bull Run*. New York, 1993

Jackson, Harry L. *First Regiment Engineer Troops P.A.C.S.: Robert E. Lee's Combat Engineers*. Louisa, Virginia, 1998

Johnston, Joseph E. *Narrative of Military Operations*. Millwood, New York, 1981

Jomini, Baron Antoine Henry de. *The Art of War*. London, 1992

Jones, John B., Earl Schenk Miers, (ed.). *A Rebel War Clerk's Diary*. New York, 1958

Katcher, Philip. *The Army of Robert E. Lee*. London, 1994

— *Sharpshooters of the Civil War*. Chicago, 2003

Krick, Robert E. L. *Staff Officers in Gray: A Biographical Register of the Staff Officers in the Army of Northern Virginia*. Chapel Hill, North Carolina, 2003

Lavender, David. *Climax at Buena Vista*. Philadelphia, 1966

Lee, Henry (Light Horse Harry). *The American Revolution in the South*. New York, 1869

Lee, Captain Robert E. *Recollections and Letters of General Robert E. Lee*. Garden City, New York, 1904

Livermore, Thomas L. *Numbers and Losses in the Civil War in America, 1861–1865*. Dayton, Ohio, 1975

Long, E. B. *The Civil War Day by Day: an Almanac 1861–1865*. New York, 1971

Longstreet, James. *From Manassas to Appomattox*. New York, 1991

Lord, Francis (ed.). *The Fremantle Diary*. Boston, 1954

Luvaas, Jay, and Nelson, Harold W. *The U.S. Army War College Guide to the Battles of Chancellorsville and Fredericksburg*. New York, 1989

McDonald, Archie P. (ed.). *Make Me a Map Of the Valley: the Civil War Journal of Stonewall Jackson's Topographer*. Dallas, Texas, 1973

McMurry, Richard M. *Two Great Rebel Armies*. Chapel Hill, North Carolina, 1989

Nevins, Allan (ed.). *Polk: The Diary of a President, 1845–1849*. New York, 1968.

Newell, Clayton R. *Lee vs. McClellan: the First Campaign*. Washington, D.C., 1996

Newton, Steven H. *Lost for the Cause: The Confederate Army in 1864*. Mason City, Iowa, 2000

Nolan, Alan T. *Lee Reconsidered: General Robert E. Lee and Civil War History*. Chapel Hill, North Carolina, 1991

Perry, John. *Lady of Arlington. The Life of Mrs. Robert E. Lee*. Sisters, Oregon, 2003

Polley, J. B. *Hood's Texas Brigade*. Dayton, Ohio, 1976

Priest, John Michael. *Nowhere to Run: The Wilderness, May 4th and 5th, 1864*. Shippensburg, Pennsylvania, 1995

— *Victory Without Triumph: The Wilderness, May 6th and 7th, 1864*. Shippensburg, Pennsylvania, 1996

Reid, J. W. *History of the Fourth Regiment S.C. Volunteers, from the Commencement of the War until Lee's Surrender*. Greenville, South Carolina, 1891

Schenk, Martin. *Up Came Hill*. Harrisburg, Pennsylvania, 1958

Scott, Winfield. *Memoirs*. New York, 1864

Sears, Stephen W. *Gettysburg*. New York, 2003

— (ed.). *The Civil War Papers of George B. McClellan*. New York, 1989

Sorrel, G. Moxley. *Recollections of a Confederate Staff Officer*. New York, 1994

Swinton, William. *Army of the Potomac*. New York, 1995

Taylor, Richard. *Destruction and Reconstruction: Personal Experiences of the Late War*. New York, 1955

Tower, R. Lockwood (ed.). *Lee's Adjutant: The Wartime Letters of Colonel Walter Herron Taylor, 1862–1865*. Columbia, South Carolina, 1995

Traas, Adrian George. *From the Golden Gate to Mexico City: the U.S. Army's Topographical Engineers in the Mexican War, 1846–1848*. Washington, D.C., 1993

Wallace, Lee A., Jr. *A Guide To Virginia Military Organizations 1861–1865*. Lynchburg, Virginia, 1986

Warner, Ezra J., *Generals in Blue: Lives of the Union Commanders*. Baton Rouge, Lousiana, 1964

White, Henry Alexander. *Robert E. Lee and the Southern Confederacy, 1807–1870*. New York, 1968

Wise, Jennings Cropper. *The Long Arm of Lee*. Lincoln, Nebraska, 1991

Woodworth, Steven E. *Davis and Lee at War*. Lawrence, Kansas, 1995

Zeh, Frederick. *An Immigrant Soldier in the Mexican War*. College Station, Texas, 1995

Philadelphia Weekly Times. The Annals of the War written by Leading Participants North and South. Dayton, Ohio, 1988 Scott, Robert *et al.* (eds.). *The War of the Rebellion: a Compilation of the Official Records of the Union and Confederate Armies*. Washington, various dates.

INDEX